The Lazarus Generation

How to Raise the Spiritually Dead

The Lazarus Generation

How to Raise the Spiritually Dead

Samuel L. Brassfield

© Copyright 1993 — Samuel L. Brassfield

All rights reserved. This book is protected under the copyright laws of the United States of America. This book may not be copied or reprinted for commercial gain or profit. The use of short quotations or occasional page copying for personal or group study is permitted and encouraged. Permission will be granted upon request. Unless otherwise identified, Scripture quotations are from the HOLY BIBLE, NEW INTERNATIONAL VERSION. Copyright © 1973, 1978, 1984 International Bible Society. Used by permission of Zondervan Bible Publishers.

Scripture marked (AMP) is taken from THE AMPLIFIED BIBLE, Old Testament copyright © 1965, 1987 by the Zondervan Corporation. The Amplified New Testament copyright © 1958, 1987 by The Lockman Foundation. Used by permission.

Scripture marked (NKJ) is taken from The Holy Bible, New King James Version. Copyright © 1982 by Thomas Nelson, Inc.

Scripture marked (TLB) is from *The Living Bible* © 1971 owned by assignment to Illinois Regional Bank, N.A., Elmhurst, IL. All rights reserved.

Emphasis in quoted Scripture is the author's own.

Take note that the name satan and related names are not capitalized. We choose not to acknowledge him, even to the point of violating grammatical rules.

Treasure House
An Imprint of
Destiny Image
P.O. Box 310
Shippensburg, PA 17257

"For where your treasure is
there will your heart be also" Matthew 6:21

ISBN 1-56043-795-2

For Worldwide Distribution
Printed in the U.S.A.

Treasure House books are available through these fine distributors outside the United States:

Christian Growth, Inc.
Jalan Kilang-Timor, Singapore 0315

Lifestream
Nottingham, England

Rhema Ministries Trading
Randburg, South Africa

Salvation Book Centre
Petaling, Jaya, Malaysia

Successful Christian Living
Capetown, Rep. of South Africa

Vision Resources
Ponsonby, Auckland, New Zealand

WA Buchanan Company
Geebung, Queensland, Australia

Word Alive
Niverville, Manitoba, Canada

Dedication

I dedicate this book to my two lovely daughters, Vanessa Renee Milligan, aged 32 years, and Suzanne Denee Myer, aged 27 years.

My daughters are pure examples of God's love and grace who lived and survived the pastor's parsonage. When I look back at what they might have seen, both in me and in the Laodicean church world, I know it was God's very own love and resurrection power that protected and sustained them through the years.

Vanessa and Suzanne have taught me so much about God the Father's love. They really didn't know it at the time, but God used them to teach me more than any higher school of learning could hope to teach a man...

I love you both!
Your Dad

Now a man named Lazarus was sick. He was from Bethany, the village of Mary and her sister Martha. This Mary, whose brother Lazarus now lay sick, was the same one who poured perfume on the Lord and wiped His feet with her hair. So the sisters sent word to Jesus, "Lord, the one you love is sick."

When He heard this, Jesus said, "This sickness will not end in death. No, it is for God's glory so that God's Son may be glorified through it." Jesus loved Martha and her sister and Lazarus. Yet when He heard that Lazarus was sick, He stayed where He was two more days.

Then He said to His disciples, "Let us go back to Judea."

"But Rabbi," they said, "a short while ago the Jews tried to stone You, and yet You are going back there?"

Jesus answered, "Are there not twelve hours of daylight? A man who walks by day will not stumble, for he sees by this world's light. It is when he walks by night that he stumbles, for he has no light."

After He had said this, He went on to tell them, "Our friend Lazarus has fallen asleep; but I am going there to wake him up."

His disciples replied, "Lord, if he sleeps, he will get better." Jesus had been speaking of his death, but His disciples thought He meant natural sleep.

So then He told them plainly, "Lazarus is dead, and for your sake I am glad I was not there, so that you may believe. But let us go to him."

Then Thomas (called Didymus) said to the rest of the disciples, "Let us also go, that we may die with Him."

On His arrival, Jesus found that Lazarus had already been in the tomb for four days. Bethany was less than two miles from Jerusalem, and many Jews had come to Martha and Mary to comfort them in the loss of their brother. When Martha heard that Jesus was coming, she went out to meet Him, but Mary stayed at home.

"Lord," Martha said to Jesus, "if You had been here, my brother would not have died. But I know that even now God will give You whatever You ask."

Jesus said to her, "Your brother will rise again."

Martha answered, "I know he will rise again in the resurrection at the last day."

Jesus said to her, "I am the resurrection and the life. He who believes in Me will live, even though he dies; and whoever lives and believes in Me will never die. Do you believe this?"

"Yes, Lord," she told Him, "I believe that You are the Christ, the Son of God, who was to come into the world."

And after she had said this, she went back and called her sister Mary aside. "The Teacher is here," she said, "and is asking for you." When Mary heard this, she got up quickly and went to Him. Now Jesus had not yet entered the village, but was still at the place where Martha had met Him. When the Jews who had been with Mary in the house, comforting her, noticed how quickly she got up and went out, they followed her, supposing she was going to the tomb to mourn there.

When Mary reached the place where Jesus was and saw Him, she fell at His feet and said, "Lord, if You had been here, my brother would not have died."

When Jesus saw her weeping, and the Jews who had come along with her also weeping, He was deeply moved in spirit and troubled. "Where have you laid him?" He asked.

"Come and see, Lord," they replied.

Jesus wept.

Then the Jews said, "See how He loved him!"

But some of them said, "Could not He who opened the eyes of the blind man have kept this man from dying?"

Jesus, once more deeply moved, came to the tomb. It was a cave with a stone laid across the entrance. "Take away the stone," He said.

"But, Lord," said Martha, the sister of the dead man, "by this time there is a bad odor, for he has been there four days."

Then Jesus said, "Did I not tell you that if you believed, you would see the glory of God?"

So they took away the stone. Then Jesus looked up and said, "Father, I thank You that You have heard Me. I knew that You always hear Me, but I said this for the benefit of the people standing here, that they may believe that You sent Me."

When He had said this, Jesus called in a loud voice, "Lazarus, come out!" The dead man came out, his hands and feet wrapped with strips of linen, and a cloth around his face.

Jesus said to them, "Take off the grave clothes and let him go."

Therefore many of the Jews who had come to visit Mary, and had seen what Jesus did, put their faith in Him. But some of them went to the Pharisees and told them what Jesus had done. Then the chief priests and the Pharisees called a meeting of the Sanhedrin.

"What are we accomplishing?" they asked. "Here is this man performing many miraculous signs. If we let Him go on like this, everyone will believe in Him, and then the Romans will come and take away both our place and our nation" (John 11:1-48).

Six days before the Passover, Jesus arrived at Bethany, where Lazarus lived, whom Jesus had raised from the dead. Here a dinner was given in Jesus' honor. Martha served, while Lazarus was among those reclining at the table with Him. Then Mary took about a pint of pure nard, an expensive perfume; she poured it on Jesus' feet and wiped His feet with her hair. And the house was filled with the fragrance of the perfume.

But one of His disciples, Judas Iscariot, who was later to betray Him, objected, "Why wasn't this perfume sold and the money given to the poor? It was worth a year's wages." He did not say this because he cared about the poor but because he was a thief; as keeper of the money bag, he used to help himself to what was put into it.

"Leave her alone," Jesus replied. "It was intended that she should save this perfume for the day of My burial. You will always have the poor among you, but you will not always have Me."

Meanwhile a large crowd of Jews found out that Jesus was there and came, not only because of Him but also to see Lazarus, whom He had raised from the dead. So the chief priests made plans to kill Lazarus as well, for on account of him many of the Jews were going over to Jesus and putting their faith in Him.

The next day the great crowd that had come for the Feast heard that Jesus was on His way to Jerusalem. They took palm branches and went out to meet Him, shouting,

"Hosanna!"

"Blessed is He who comes in the name of the Lord!"

"Blessed is the King of Israel!"

Jesus found a young donkey and sat upon it, as it is written,

"Do not be afraid, O Daughter of Zion; see, your king is coming, seated on a donkey's colt."

At first His disciples did not understand all this. Only after Jesus was glorified did they realize that these things had been written about Him and that they had done these things to Him.

Now the crowd that was with Him when He called Lazarus from the tomb and raised him from the dead continued to spread the word. Many people, because they had heard that He had given this miraculous sign, went out to meet Him. So the Pharisees said to one another, "See, this is getting us nowhere. Look how the whole world has gone after Him!" (John 12:1-19)

I tell you the truth, whoever hears My word and believes Him who sent Me has eternal life and will not be condemned; he has crossed over from death to life. I tell you the truth, a time is coming and has now come when the dead will hear the voice of the Son of God and those who hear will live. For as the Father has life in Himself, so He has granted the Son to have life in Himself. And He has given Him authority to judge because He is the Son of Man.

Do not be amazed at this, for a time is coming when all who are in their graves will hear His voice (John 5:24-28).

This is the Lazarus Generation!

Contents

	Introduction	xix
Chapter 1	Lazarus Was Sick!	1
Chapter 2	Religious People Will Stone You	7
Chapter 3	The Friend Factor (the "I Am" Factor)	15
Chapter 4	Excerpts From a Dead Man's Diary	27
Chapter 5	Prodigal Preachers Produce Prodigal Parsonages and P.K.'s	43
Chapter 6	The Prodigal Pew, Pee-u!	49
Chapter 7	I'm Glad I Was Not There…Let's Go!	57
Chapter 8	"Let *Us* Also Go!"	61

Chapter 9	Jesus, Three; Lazarus, Four!	63
Chapter 10	Look Who's Pouting Now!	71
Chapter 11	Look Who's Believing Now!	79
Chapter 12	Jesus Is Lord!	85
Chapter 13	The Resurrection Factor	89
Chapter 14	They Wept; He Wept!	93
Chapter 15	"Take Away the Stone!"	99
Chapter 16	He Came Out Alive—But Bound	103
Chapter 17	First Aid (Love) for Lazarus!	109
Chapter 18	Believer or "Rat-Fink" Religionist?	129
Chapter 19	Prophecy Fulfilled— The Restoration of the Rascals	133
Chapter 20	Will Jesus Come to the Dinner?	139
Chapter 21	A Final Word on the Final Restoration	147
Chapter 22	A Last Word on the Restoration of Lazarus	153
Chapter 23	Remember Rahab's Red Ribbon?	163
Chapter 24	The Finished Product	179

Introduction

But...this brother of yours was dead and is alive again; he was lost and is found (Luke 15:32).

I tell you the truth, whoever hears My word and believes Him who sent Me has eternal life and will not be condemned; he has crossed over from death to life. I tell you the truth, a time is coming and has now come when the dead will hear the voice of the Son of God and those who hear will live. For as the Father has life in Himself, so He has granted the Son to have life in Himself. And He has given Him authority to judge because He is the Son of Man. Do not be amazed at this, for a time is coming when all who are in their graves will hear His voice and come out—*those who have done good will rise to live, and those who have done evil will rise to be condemned* (John 5:24-29).

Never in the history of this world has there been such a time as today! Or has there been?

It is said that history always repeats itself. I believe it just has! We are now living in the same conditions that are recounted in our history books and, moreover, in God's Word. Yes, the Bible says, "As it was in the days of Noah, so it will be at the coming of the Son of Man" (Mt. 24:37).

What were the conditions in Noah's time? People were eating, drinking, marrying, and giving in marriage until the flood came and destroyed that entire generation. They were not aware of their fate until it was too late! Yet, Noah had preached righteousness for 120 years. God was speaking but nobody was listening.

We are now living in the time foretold in the Bible: the time of the coming of the Son of Man! However, God's judgment this time will be *fire*, not *water*. We can also expect to see righteousness begin to prevail as Jesus plans to return to set up His earthly Kingdom, which will culminate in the end of the rule of all sin and rebellion on the earth. Yes, we are now living in the time of total restoration of all things (see Acts 3:19-21): restoration of righteousness, holiness, joy, peace, and much, much more! As the flood in Noah's time cleansed the earth of all wickedness, rebellion, and sin, so shall God's refining fire cleanse the Church and the world of all unrighteousness.

Before He pours out His final judgment to rid the world of satan and sin, His first and foremost aim is to restore the Body of Christ, the Church. Then, and only then, can He restore the earth and reap a world harvest in this last great gathering of souls. Yes, history has repeated itself. We are back to where the world was before Noah and his family entered the ark—before they were saved to start a new world order in righteousness, ruled by God's love and grace.

As we will recall, that particular new beginning and generation didn't follow after righteousness and God's plan either. Consequently, they too went right back to where they started. "Now the earth was corrupt in God's sight and was full of violence" (Gen. 6:11). Our present generation has repeated history to the point where we are just as wicked as they were. The parable of the prodigal son, as found in Luke 15, is a perfect picture of our own generation. Even though the parable is a graphic picture of a desperate, degenerate, detestable, deplorable, wayward son (generation), yet there is *hope*! (I know those were a lot of D's, but we are truly failing the grade in our generation.) Yes, there was *hope* for the prodigal son and there is *hope* for this, the Lazarus Generation—this terminal generation!

The prodigal son was in such a degenerate condition that the Bible says he "was dead" (Lk. 15:24,32). Now he was not dead physically, but spiritually and emotionally; he was dead in terms of his relationship and fellowship with his family. The father said, "…this brother of yours was dead and is alive again; he was lost and is found" (v. 32). I believe that just as the prodigal son was dead, so is this Lazarus Generation—spiritually, emotionally; without fellowship with God the Father and His Son.

It looked as if this prodigal son would die in a foreign country, totally destitute, living in the pigpen of sin. He squandered his wealth in wild living and then found himself in a severe famine that engulfed the whole country. Not until he realized his need—filling his stomach with pig slop and receiving no help from anyone—did he remember his father and come to his senses, saying this:

> …*"How many of my father's hired men have food to spare, and here I am starving to death! I will set out and go back to my father and say to him: Father, I have sinned against heaven and against you. I am no longer worthy to be called your son; make me like one of your hired men"* (Luke 15:14-19).

All it took to change his seemingly *hopeless* fate was to be remorseful, to repent, and to return to his father! We know what happened upon his return to his father—his father responded with great joy, compassion, and *total restoration* for his son! The prodigal was restored to full sonship in his *father's* house. I emphasize the word *father* so much in this paragraph because he truly was a father first! The prodigal's father is our Father! His basic attribute is Father God—Abba Father! In the restoration of all things today we are seeing a new and true understanding of God, our Father, revealed to His children—a truth that we have neither seen nor understood until now!

A joyous celebration ensued as the fattened calf was prepared. The sound of music and dancing filled the father's house. Such celebration! Quickly! Bring the best robe and put it on him. Put a ring on his finger and sandals on his feet. Bring the fattened calf and kill it. Why? " 'For this son of mine was dead and is alive again; he was lost and is found'…" (Lk. 15:24). I believe with all of my heart that the total restoration of the Body of Christ could be a quick work if we would simply see our present condition and repent! The question of whether or not the Father will forgive and restore the prodigal church member is not an issue. Nor is it a question of whether or not the Father will forgive and restore the backslider, be it your son or mine, a prodigal preacher or preacher's son, a deacon or his daughter. No, revival is not being hindered in Heaven, but here on earth! The

Father is ready to *restore* and *revive* if we will only *realize* and *repent*!

Neither is it a matter of finances that keeps us from reaping a worldwide harvest. The prodigal's father still had plenty to give his returned son: "Kill the fattened calf!" The Word says, "But a sinner's wealth is stored up for the righteous" (Prov. 13:22b). It's stored up for the righteous? That's right! I believe that the Father is just waiting for the right time to release all of that wealth to the Church, in order that it might reap the final harvest. Yes, the Church must use that wealth not for its own lusts, but for reaping the harvest. James 5:1-20 tells us that the cries of the harvesters have reached the ears of the Lord Almighty and that the wicked rich have fattened themselves in the day of slaughter. But then James continues to say to the brothers, to the Church, "Be patient, then, brothers, until the Lord's coming..." (5:7). He tells us to persevere, to be patient, and to look at Job and what the Lord finally did. "...The Lord is full of compassion and mercy" (5:11), just as the father was toward his prodigal son in Luke's Gospel.

Revival is very, very close—but there is a real danger that deserves our closest attention. I feel that perhaps this danger is the reason God had me write this book, *The Lazarus Generation*. It was not to present His promise to send revival and to restore all things, but to warn the Church that God loves the sinner, the worst prodigal you could ever imagine. He loves the lost nations, this mostly "gentile" world so very, very much that, if He must, He will go to extreme measures to reach and win this spiritually dead generation.

You ask, "So what does that have to do with me?" It has virtually everything to do with you, my friend! You see, in the parable of the prodigal, the prodigal himself was repentant and the father so full of compassion that he was more than willing to forgive and forget his son's past. However, there is one other character in this parable whom we haven't discussed: the older brother. Without doubt, the older brother in this story represents an attitude so prevalent in the Church today that it's frightening! This attitude is a real problem and God is about to address it "big time"!

The household began to celebrate as soon as the father said, "…'Quick! Bring the best robe and put it on him. Put a ring on his finger and sandals on his feet. Bring the fattened calf and kill it. Let's have a feast and celebrate. For this son of mine was dead and is alive again; he was lost and is found'…" (Lk. 15:22-24). At that moment, the older son was coming home from the field. As he got closer to the house, he heard music and dancing and asked one of the servants what was going on. When the servant gave him the good news that his brother was home, safe and sound, what was the older brother's response? The Bible says that he "became angry and refused to go in" (Lk. 15:28). Can you imagine becoming angry when your own brother is back home safe and your father is so happy?

Let's look at what I believe to be the crux of this book: how we, the present church world, will respond to the news about this Lazarus Generation—this low-down, low-life, pigpen-party-type of people—as they start repenting and returning to the Church. Are we like the older brother? Or are we like the father? We have a choice to make; let us choose wisely! After the older son threw such a fit of anger, pouting and refusing to come into the house, the father went out to him and pleaded with his older son. Our heavenly Father is so very happy that this dying and dead generation—this generation rightly tagged as "terminal"—will be raised up to new life before Jesus returns. Just as Jesus raised Lazarus from the grave after four days, so will He raise up this spiritually dead generation and allow them to return to His house where He will treat them as first-class citizens, with all "family rights" fully restored.

He will do this with or without this present Laodicean church world's permission! The older brother represents this Pharisee-ridden church world, which is so full of self-righteousness that it will be a miracle of miracles if they accept what God is about to do!

The father heard the older son out, yet he said, "But we had to celebrate and be glad, because this brother of yours was dead and is alive again; he was lost and is found" (Lk. 15:32). The older son had just denied being related to his brother in verse 30, saying, "But when this son of yours who has squandered your property with prostitutes comes home, you kill the fattened calf for him!" He was pouting, refusing to claim kinship to his brother, arguing with the father, self-righteously defending his own selfish pride; yet hearing his loving father say, "Please, son, all I have is yours. Won't you come in and celebrate with me on this great occasion?" The big question is this: Did the older son ever go in? The Bible does not answer that. The greater question today is this: Will you go in? Will you celebrate with the Father and His household as this dead, stinking, rotting generation of prodigal children returns to the Father?

Are you ready for this Lazarus Generation to be raised from spiritual death and to come walking into your church with their graveclothes still on? Like it or not, the Lazarus Generation is coming! The way you respond will determine if you will have a church or a mortuary; revival or survival; a great move of God and His presence or "The Glory Departed" written above your doors!

This book may shake your present attitude and theology. God, the Father, is about to do something so radical that, if you are not warned about it before it happens, it might just blow you away! So get ready; here it comes: the Lazarus Generation!

Chapter 1

Lazarus Was Sick!

Now a man named Lazarus was sick. He was from Bethany, the village of Mary and her sister Martha. This Mary, whose brother Lazarus now lay sick, was the same one who poured perfume on the Lord and wiped His feet with her hair. So the sisters sent word to Jesus, "Lord, the one You love is sick." When He heard this, Jesus said, "This sickness will not end in death. No, it is for God's glory so that God's Son may be glorified through it." Jesus loved Martha and her sister and Lazarus. Yet when He heard that Lazarus was sick, He stayed where He was two more days (John 11:1-6).

How many times in the last few days have you said, or heard someone else say, "Boy, we sure live in a sick society!" Not too long ago it was reported throughout the U.S. that a young man's neighbors had been smelling a terrible odor coming from his apartment. They discovered it was the smell of rotting human remains that he had left in cooking pots after he had killed, dismembered, cooked, and eaten these people! Yes, I said he had been eating his murdered victims. If that was not bad enough, the real atrocity was he had been doing it for years and getting away with it!

A sick society? You better believe it! But what is worse (if worse is possible) is the fact that thousands of this type of people are loose in our society! The news media was reported to have said, "Certainly this young man is *totally insane!*" Yes, we live in an insane, inhumane world that seems to be getting worse, not better! It's real sick, folks, just as Lazarus was. As a matter of fact, our generation has been called "the terminal generation." I would have agreed with that statement except the Holy Spirit spoke to me about this Lazarus Generation and gave me very good cause to believe we have *hope* (and not just more dope)! This *hope* is found in only one person.

"You mean the *hope* for this whole sick society rests with a single person, Preacher?"

Yes, I really do mean that.

"Well, please inform me who it is."

I'm glad you asked. His name is *Jesus*. Yes, sweet Jesus *is* (and I really mean *He is*) our only *hope*!

Lazarus Was Sick!

I know this for a fact because I hear and see so many who have either given up hope or who are so puzzled about how to find the answer that they wonder if there even is one! One Sunday morning when I was serving as senior pastor at Church on the Rock in Grand Junction, Colorado, a precious mother came to the front during the altar service.

"Altar what?"

Yes, I said "altar service"! If you don't have one during every single service at your church, then you better find a church that does have a time when you can come to Jesus. I want you to know this, dear reader. If your pastor doesn't give an invitation for salvation, healing, deliverance, baptism in the Holy Spirit, and rededication in your church, you need to pray for that person, for you are getting "ripped off," spiritually speaking.

However, let's go back to this puzzled mother's sad scenario. Here was her story to me:

> Pastor, I've just returned from my daughter's. She called and asked me and her grandmother to come over to her city because the Welfare Department would not allow her to come over to Grand Junction with the kids. When we arrived at her home (if you can call it that, for it was a total mess), I found out, Pastor, that she had no money and no food for her six children because the kids had stolen her food stamps ($300 worth

or so) and given them to all the neighbors. Pastor, my daughter told me that she had just wrecked her car, having run it into the river, and that she was injured and hurting real bad. (She had no license or insurance on the car because of too many citations for "Driving under the influence.") Also, she is an alcoholic, has been married several times, and has had several children by several men. Pastor, she said she needed $275, and I asked her why. She said, "So I can have an abortion, Mama, for I had to sell my body for food for the kids." She told me this while her body shook involuntarily, because of the internal injuries she got from the accident when she ran her car into the river.

Oh, my Lord in Heaven, is there no end? Dear reader, this precious mother then told me:

Pastor B., I just didn't know what to do! So I got into my car and drove back to Grand Junction. Pastor, was I wrong? Oh Pastor, I do have some good news to tell you. My son who is in the state prison is really doing well and will soon be released to a prison with lesser security.

He had turned his life over to the Lord and the 50-year term he was serving at the Colorado State Prison had just recently been reduced. By the way, her other son was released from a California prison to return to his mother also—but not quite like his brother. This

34-year-old returned home where he died of AIDS. However, he gave his heart to the Lord in one of our services just a few months before he died. Praise the Lord!

Now I ask you, do you think our Lazarus Generation is sick, or what? The Bible says that Lazarus was "sick" in John 11:1, but in verse 2 it says that he "now lay sick" or, in other words, he got sicker. So his two sisters sent word of his illness to Jesus and said, "Lord, the one You love is sick" (v. 3). Jesus loves this Lazarus Generation, in spite of its terminal sickness!

Next we see Jesus' response to the news of His friend's sickness. "This sickness will not end in death. No, it is for God's glory so that God's Son may be glorified through it" (Jn. 11:4).

"You've got to be kidding! Dear Jesus! Do you mean that God the Father and Jesus will get *glory* from sickness?"

That's what He said! Moreover, when He heard the news, "He stayed where He was two more days. Then He said to His disciples, 'Let us go back to Judea' " (Jn. 11:6-7).

Jesus was and is the "bottom line" on sickness, disease, and death! He had, and still has, control over "*all* the power of the enemy"! (See Luke 10:19.) That hasn't changed a bit.

We may think that our generation, which is called "the Lazarus Generation," is very sick and will shortly die if something doesn't happen soon. But I'm here to tell you that Jesus isn't worried to death; He isn't puzzled, paranoid, or as panicky as we might be! I'm also here to tell you that the Father and Jesus will soon get untold glory and be glorified beyond reason, *by raising Lazarus from the dead*! Praise the Lord!

You see, the sicker Lazarus gets, the greater the glory to God! God is allowing our society, social services, and worldly systems (governments) to run their course. He is letting everyone and everything do their thing. He's letting our so-called advanced school systems, run by New Agers and socialistic, humanistic, communistic, atheistic, and every other "silly-istic" type of people, to run their course. Believe me, it's true! Just about the time (and that's about now) we think there's absolutely and positively no hope, Jesus will come and save this "terminal generation." In fact, it's already begun! Jesus is now on His way back to Judea—back to where Lazarus is very sick and dying; back to your world and mine. He is returning to the gutters and ghettos and to the pimps and penthouses! He is coming back to the "druggers," "dopers," and "ropers," to the white collars, blue collars, and no collars. Every sector of society and every nation on earth will soon see Jesus at work (through His Church) in this seemingly God-forsaken generation of ours! Get ready; Jesus is coming to the graveside service of Lazarus, not to mourn his passing, but to call him forth from his tomb! Hallelujah!

Chapter 2

Religious People Will Stone You

Religion Will Kill You

Then He said to His disciples, "Let us go back to Judea." "But Rabbi," they said, "a short while ago the Jews tried to stone You, and yet You are going back there?" Jesus answered, "Are there not twelve hours of daylight? A man who walks by day will not stumble, for he sees by this world's light" (John 11:7-9).

When Jesus said to His disciples, "Let us go back to Judea," He quickly got His disciples' attention! By this time in their dealings with the "religious folks," they had discovered this fact: *Religious people will stone you and religion will **kill you dead**!* (Excuse the double dying, but if some of the religious people I know could kill you twice, believe me, they would!)

Anytime you decide to go into the "raising-of-the-dead ministry," you will surely raise the "religious spirits" too! Every religious spirit in a hundred-mile radius will rise up against you. Since they tried, and succeeded, in killing Jesus, they will surely try to kill you too. But remember, only by God's permission were they able to crucify our Lord. It was in the plan! (Read about it in Acts 4:24-28.)

" 'But Rabbi,' they said, 'a short while ago the Jews tried to stone You, and yet You are going back there?' " (Jn. 11:8) I just love the reply Jesus gave them:

Jesus answered, "Are there not twelve hours of daylight? A man who walks by day will not stumble, for he sees by this world's light (John 11:9).

Here is what I think He meant. I paraphrase:

Look, guys, there are 12 hours of daylight. A man who walks in revelation knowledge and wisdom has been in prayer since "early" this morning. The preachers who have been in fellowship with the Father for hours before everyone else has gotten up—the five-fold-ministry-gift guys who are in the Word of God; those pastors who believe in a "word of knowledge" or "word of wisdom" and "distinguishing between spirits"; those guys who dare to say, "The Holy Ghost spoke to me and said…"; those preachers who still believe in miracles, signs, and wonders, who still believe in the "supernatural" and who know who they are in Christ Jesus—they will not be afraid of any religious spirit or of any person who goes with those spirits! Period!

Jesus was saying just that! He also was saying this: The only time you have to worry is when you don't believe what He just said and still walk in ignorance (the dark) of what His ministry was and still is about!

I'm going to get bold at this juncture. I dare say that if you call yourself a "five-fold ministry gift" according to First Corinthians 12:27-28 and Ephesians 4:8-13, or you know someone who claims to be one of these gifts to the Body of Christ, but neither of you practice what I have just paraphrased, oh friend, I feel very sorry for you!

"Why do you say that?"

I'm glad you asked! You see, dear reader, if you don't believe these things like Jesus taught and practiced them, you are in *big* trouble in these last days as a minister!

That's right—you better *minister*! To minister is to *meet* people's *needs*, and that means even ministering to our "Lazarus" folks!

"Oh, those poor people who smell of death? Who are 'dead'? Who are full of AIDS? Full of disease? Full of dope? Full of drink and stink?"

Yes, it includes all of those and more! Oh, you don't think that Lazarus stank? Why do you think Lazarus' two sisters didn't want to roll the stone away? It would take a family member or a real (true) friend to stand the odor of a dead man's rotten flesh. You might be there now, in the bedroom of a loved one who is dying with AIDS or cancer or something else. I know it's a bad smell, but please do what Jesus tells you! Help Him by rolling away the stone! He is here, back in Judea, to raise up your brother Lazarus. That's why He risked the stone-throwing of the "religious" and died at the hands of "religion"—so He might have resurrection power to raise your dead!

For your sake as well as for mine, dear minister, please, walk in the light with which Christ has called you (see 1 John 1:6-7). Don't be afraid of those religious controlling spirits in your denomination or your church. Instead, fear allowing someone or something like that to keep you from *ministering* to your dear sheep—to the Lazarus Generation! Oh, be certain that they stink. But believe me, so do those religious folks who throw stones at Jesus and His disciples! God says those are the ones who really stink, and He is just about fed up with them. So watch out, all religious folks and religions! Here comes Jesus with His disciples back to Judea where their friend Lazarus is dead. Jesus is coming to "wake him up"!

Remember what Jesus said? "You are the light of the world" (Mt. 5:14a). If you don't walk in the light, how do you expect the blind of this world to see Jesus? They won't, so light up! Light up your city, your state, and your world. Jesus has called you to bring the light (Jesus) to your generation, no matter how sad, sick, sorry, and sinful it is!

"Our friend Lazarus has fallen asleep [physically then, but spiritually today]," Jesus said, "but I am [the I Am that I Am] is going there to wake him up" (Jn. 11:11). Praise the Lord! The "*I am* the light of the world" (Jn. 8:12) is going to the dark graveside of His friend Lazarus (who sleeps in darkness) to wake him up! What a positive, powerful, faith statement that is!

How many of you preachers, teachers, and church folks remember what Jesus taught in Matthew 5:11-16? This book is here to remind you, lest you forget and get lost in the shuffle of the new things God our Father is doing!

Blessed are you when people insult you, persecute you and falsely say all kinds of evil against you because of Me. Rejoice and be glad, because great is your reward in heaven, for in the same way they persecuted the prophets who were before you. You are the salt of the earth. But if the salt loses its saltiness, how can it be made salty again? It is no longer good for anything, except to be thrown out and trampled by men. You are the light of the world. A city on a hill cannot be hidden. Neither do people light a lamp and put it under a bowl. Instead they put it on its stand, and it gives light to everyone in the house. In the same way, let your light shine before men, that they may see your good deeds and praise your Father in heaven (Matthew 5:11-16).

Now that you have read the bottom line on "light"; "salt"; and "city," are you blessed because religious people are insulting you, persecuting you, and falsely saying all kinds of nasty, evil things against you because of Jesus in you? Or are you like the salt that has lost its saltiness and is good for *nothing*? Are you a good-for-nothing preacher or churchgoer who has either let the light go totally out or hidden it under some religious or demoralized, demonic, demolished denominationalism? Have you put it under a denomination that's so sectarian and biased, bigoted, and bigheaded, that you won't budge? (By the way, one of the definitions of bias, other than prejudice, is "the tendency of a bowl to swerve"! It's "a peculiarity in the shape of a bowl that causes it to swerve when rolled on the green" [green ware].[1]) Maybe a better definition is this one: "light under a bowl." Perhaps you are that person Jesus spoke of here in Matthew 5:15, who has hidden his light under a bowl that is out of round with what God, the Holy Spirit is, doing today.

Remember, you are the light of the world. Like it or not, all the world has is you and me. So let that light shine for Jesus. Will you be His witness? Will you?

---

1. *Webster's Ninth New Collegiate Dictionary* (Springfield, Massachusetts: Merriam-Webster Inc., Publishers, 1988).

Chapter 3

The Friend Factor (the "I Am" Factor)

*After He had said this, He went on to tell them, "Our friend Lazarus has fallen asleep; but **I am** going there to wake him up." His disciples replied, "Lord, if he sleeps, he will get better." Jesus had been speaking of his death, but His disciples thought He meant natural sleep. So then He told them plainly, "Lazarus is dead, and for your sake **I am** glad **I was** not there, so that you may believe. But **let us** go to him"* (John 11:11-15).

Jesus had given them the Sermon on the Mount, "You are the light of the world—A city on a hill cannot be hidden" re-run. Apparently they missed the point of His whole message in Matthew 5. (I hope you didn't.) Time is of the essence today for "our friend Lazarus" is dead! This generation is as spiritually dead as any other generation in the history of this world.

Jesus described and compared Lazarus' physical death to a spiritual death that would occur in a time and generation then unknown to mankind—ours. Yes, Church, He was speaking to our generation, preparing us for His return to earth. Moreover, He showed us His "resurrection power" that can raise up from a "spiritual death" a generation of spiritual Lazaruses, who by all standards are totally, spiritually dead!

I am presenting this to you as the "absolute truth"! Whatever is in the Word of God as a natural happening also occurs in the spiritual sense! First the natural, then the spiritual, just as it was with the first Adam and the second Adam, Jesus. We, the Lazarus Generation, or the last generation, represent in the spiritual what the first Lazarus represented in the natural.

Some still don't believe it, though. They say, "We will try this new drug on the *masses* of AIDS patients." Just as the disciples thought, "Lord, if he sleeps, he will get better" (Jn. 11:12). No, my friend,

The Friend Factor (the "I Am" Factor)

this situation will not get better by its own power. The problem with AIDS, cancer, spirits of infirmity, diseases of all descriptions, drugs, and alcohol, won't get any better or go away on their own! Abortion, resulting from a morally "loose life style," won't solve the problem of teenage pregnancies. We are dealing with a sin factor, not a fun factor. It is written in the Word of God: "...Let us eat and drink; for tomorrow we shall die" (Is. 22:13 KJV). How true that is, if we don't grasp the faith factor and find the I Am factor before it becomes the too-late factor! It is already too late for the many who died of AIDS without the I Am factor, who is the friend factor of this Lazarus Generation!

Why am I speaking so much of AIDS? As leprosy was a physical and spiritual type of sin, so today AIDS is a physical and spiritual type of sin!

AIDS represents the spiritual type of sin that has plagued the world since almost the beginning of time. However, the AIDS factor can still be eradicated through the faith factor in the Jesus factor! Praise the Lord! But I remind you again, only in the Jesus factor will AIDS be eliminated from this world. AIDS is a worldwide epidemic; however, Jesus and His Church will also soon be a worldwide epidemic! Before long you will see and hear of the masses of people coming to Jesus in countries like Uganda, Africa—a war-torn nation where AIDS is killing as many as 50 percent of the population of some villages. In the next few years you will hear reports of mass healings from AIDS. It will take place by none other than the friend factor in Jesus, a true friend "who sticks closer than a brother" (Prov. 18:24). He will not fail to return to Judea, nor will He be afraid to face the stones of the religious and the worldwide religions to get to where Lazarus lays in spiritual death!

Have you realized yet that we are the only Jesus this world will see (before He actually returns)? We, the Church factor, are the light of this world! We are His hands, His feet, His love, mercy, and grace. We are His eyes, to see the lost and dying; His heart (His body), to save Lazarus from total destruction in hell. We must, by the power of Jesus' name and faith in that name, go back to Judea (the graveside of Lazarus) because we love him and because he is our friend. We must loose him from his "spiritual tomb" of death!

Where is Judea? It is anywhere you find a person of the Lazarus Generation! Judea is right there in your own hometown, city, or megaplex—New York, Los Angeles, Dallas, Phoenix, or Philadelphia. He may be entombed in a gay bar or in a beer joint. He will surely be found in a porno shop, or an XXX-rated movie house. She may be in a city park, strung out on booze and drugs, or in a crisis pregnancy center, abortion clinic, city hall, city jail, state prison, or state hospital. He could even be under a local bridge. That's where we found one.

He was from Michigan, 33 years old, cold, without food and without any money to buy some. One of the men invited him to a service at Church on the Rock—a church that caters to the Lazarus Generation. There the young man responded to the altar call.

This young man gave his heart *again* to the Lord in recommitment and deliverance. He had once known the Lord in a very real way, but something had happened to cause him to fall. I find this to be true in almost every case that we deal with now days. (I have more to say in a later chapter about the "reasons" for backsliding or falling out of fellowship.)

Then a strange and wonderful thing happened. The young man was so happy and thankful to Jesus for allowing him to return home that he hardly knew what to do. The Holy Spirit spoke to my spirit and said, "Now, have all the people come up and start stuffing money into the bib of his smelly, dirty overalls." So that's what I did. Wow! What a response. They stuffed him full of money till his pockets wouldn't hold any more—hundreds of dollars.

The Holy Spirit then told me that the young man had been such a giver himself (he had the gift of giving) that he had literally given all he had many times. Unfortunately, people had used, misused, and abused him. So the Holy Spirit had me say these words to him: "Say, 'I am a giver.' " The young man's eyes lit up; he gleamed with glee and said emphatically, "I am a giver." Then the Holy Spirit told me to tell him: "Now say, 'I am a receiver.' " When I did that, it was quite a different story.

The Holy Spirit always knows just the right things to say to meet our every need. This young man had felt unworthy all his life: "I'm not worthy. I'm no good. I'm a bad person, so I can't possibly be worthy of receiving anything good from God or man!" He had been told that lie by his parents, his friends, and the devil, the father of lies. I begged him to say, "I am a receiver," but he only broke down in tears. He wept and wept and I hugged him and held him. Then the Holy Spirit prompted me to say, "Son, you must also be a receiver, for all of that money must convince you that you are loved and are worthy to receive and not just give." Oh, I can't tell you how wonderful God is, and how at that moment the whole church was weeping along with that young man. He was so overwhelmed by God the Father's love and grace shown to him through God's people! Words can't describe the experience. You would have had to witness it yourself to feel the emotion.

All of a sudden the young man said to me, "Pastor, I have something for you, sir." I really wondered

The Friend Factor (the "I Am" Factor)

what it could be. With the appearance of his clothes, hat, and shoes, what could he possibly give that would be of interest to me? What a shock I got. He had on all of the clothes that he owned, including a coat and an old, smelly, dirty vest. He took off that old checkered vest of many colors. (That's what he called his vest: "Joseph's coat of many colors.") He took it off and said, "Pastor, I must give you this coat."

Did you see that? This Lazarus Generation does have *hope*. They do have something to give. I discovered that night that the Church can learn a valuable lesson from this so-called "terminal" generation. This young man had shown more love and giving power than many satisfied saints who sit on pews and do nothing but grumble.

Finally, here is the wonderful part. This young man was not satisfied with just receiving a renewed relationship with the Father and all that money without giving back something in return to God, to show his love and gratitude. For those who are forgiven much, show much love and gratitude (see Lk. 7:47). The young man then said to me, "Pastor, ever since I can remember I have had this special gift that God gave me. Sir, every time I sit down at the piano, it is like it almost plays itself and only uses my fingers, or something like that. Pastor, may I play the piano for you and your church?" Well, what was I to do? It occurred to me that he just might make a fool out of himself and everyone else. Then the Holy Spirit said to me, "Let him do it." What happened in those next few minutes was more wonderful than almost anything else I had ever seen in a church service. When that young man began to play the piano, it seemed as if all of Heaven came down. Oh, such sweet music from greasy, grimy hands, we had never heard. He played a concert concerto extraordinaire! Beethoven or Bach would have been proud to have had a student with such a gift.

It's surprising to see who walks into your services when you preach and practice unconditional love. If you will open up your doors to the Lazarus Generation, you will be the winner in your city. You will begin to do the work of God for this hour and have that *city* church that God is planting in every city, large or small.

Another example in a subsequent service was an old "bum." He was dirty, ragged, and torn. One of our ladies was walking downtown and saw him passing by. The Holy Spirit told her to give him some lunch money. She then called me at the office on Saturday morning and told me this story "So, Pastor Brassfield, I did it. And as I walked away, the Spirit said, 'Tell him, God bless you.' So I did." (Please,

The Friend Factor (the "I Am" Factor)

folks, *obey the Holy Spirit*! He is your guide to this Lazarus Generation's salvation.) She explained that the man started to walk away, stopped, turned back, and told her that he too was a Christian and had several college degrees, but was so ashamed because he had become an alcoholic. He said, "Oh, how I want to be delivered from it." She invited him to our Sunday morning service, and one of our men went by to pick him up and brought him to church. Did you notice that? She invited him and someone brought him to church.

You must reach out and *bring* them. Don't just hope that they will come to your church. You must go and bring them to the banquet table of the Lord. Compel them to enter to the table of the Lord! Search the highways, byways, and hedges till His house is full.

Only then are you at liberty to build bigger churches. Don't build bigger barns without people to put in them. Win the lost at any cost! Many churches build the building at any cost and let the lost go to hell. We have far too many barns with too few people in them; they're like "BB's in a barrel." Those barns will remain barns as long as we continue our prayerlessness and depend upon our "Barbies," barbecues, and booze (so-called church socials) to keep our churches together. (By "Barbies" I mean the toys that keep us from God's Word and fellowship. They can be just about anything you can imagine.)

Let me continue on this theme for a moment. In the past few years I've seen and heard it all about many dear preachers from every kind of denominational background. Friend, we need to get rid of our "Barbie doll" sins, or whatever we play with on the sly. It could be a real, in-the-flesh "Barbie" or a paper doll on a pornographic page or screen. It really makes no difference to God; they are both sin. Some may call it a weakness, hang-up, or whatever. But remember this, my friend, God calls it *sin*.

Preacher or not, you will get caught. God sees our sin, even if no one else does. Many have played the "Barbie" game quite well, till now! "But now you have no excuse," says the sovereign God!

Here is a warning to all shepherds, evangelists, teachers, and church people at large: Get rid of your toys! It's no wonder that we don't have signs and wonders in our services anymore. Awake, all you who slumber; Christ is at the door! He is here *first* to clean up all the garbage in His Church—to get His people to return to Him and to seek His face, not His hand!

Oh, church of Laodicea, "You say, 'I am rich; I have acquired wealth and do not need a thing.' But you do not realize that you are wretched, pitiful,

The Friend Factor (the "I Am" Factor)

poor, blind and naked" (Rev. 3:17). That's not the worst of it, though. Jesus said in the preceding verse, "So, because you are lukewarm—neither hot nor cold—I am [the I Am factor] about to spit you out of My mouth" (Rev. 3:16). Remember, the dispensationalists said it: "We are now in the Laodicea church period." Just get ready, then, for Jesus' prophecy to be fulfilled in this very hour! Some may not believe that there is a returning of the prophetic voice, the spirit of prophecy, but they cannot deny that Jesus is a true prophet!

It's so very critical that the whole Body of Christ know for sure what the Spirit says to the Church today through His prophets.

"Oh, you mean they didn't disappear with the first century church?"

No! They're still around and will soon begin to prophesy as never before—by book and by mouth.

In John 11:14 Jesus said, "Lazarus is dead." He told them plainly. I, too, have been "plain" with you, that you might realize the seriousness of this book's message. Lazarus is dead—your generation and mine is spiritually dead. Our only *hope* is to join forces with the Holy Ghost and invade this Lazarus Generation with the power of Pentecost plus! By *plus* I mean we are destined for a new *double anointing* of the Spirit that we have never before seen or heard!

First, though, we must deal with the real issue at hand: getting the Church cleaned up, prayed up, and filled up with the Holy Spirit so we can do the job He has called us to, which is to *win this whole world* for Jesus! Hallelujah!

Before I leave the subject of death, for Lazarus is dead, I want you to read for yourselves what depths of death that this last generation has fallen into. The next chapter consists of a young man's notes, poems, and journal entries that he wrote several years ago. The Holy Spirit called it "Excerpts From a Dead Man's Diary" as I read them. The depth of darkness in these items is beyond words! Lazarus is really dead, dear saint!

Will you go with Jesus to your Judea? Will you help? Do we, His "modern-day disciples" really believe Him? Do we believe Him when He says that this is the last generation, the final one on earth, before He returns to earth?

Chapter 4

Excerpts From a Dead Man's Diary

Some time ago one of our young men came to visit my office for a number of reasons. One was to join our fellowship and another was to ask me, as his pastor, to perform his wedding. I know now that he was there for yet another reason. This young man showed me some poems he had written, and out of that meeting came a realization of just how spiritually dead is this generation of young people we have produced. They know absolutely nothing about the love, mercy, and power of the Holy Spirit—all the things Jesus is about. I want you to know this, though: They are seriously searching for absolute truth about life, God, and more! Generally, they either don't see or can't find a place or church where they can get answers to all their questions—the great questions of life. "Who am I? Where in the world am I going?"

If they can't find those answers in their churches, their own homes, or where they are supposed to, then they look elsewhere for their answers. They turn to their friends and discover that they too are seeking truth about life. So on and on it goes—till it ends up in a web of death. It's a death of deaths that even makes physical death seem a sweet release.

I'm afraid it's that time, Church. That's why this generation is called the Lazarus Generation. All they know is drugs, gangs, murder, rape, abortion, and AIDS! "O wretched man that I am! who shall deliver me from the body of this death? (Rom. 7:24 KJV) It was even better stated in the New International Version: "What a wretched man I am! *Who* will rescue me from this body of death?"

"Well, who is it, Preacher? Tell me quick, before I die!"

Let me now tell you! Go back to Romans 7:25 and read the first part. "Thanks be to God—through Jesus Christ our Lord!" For God the Father, your Father, gave His Son, Jesus, to die on the cross of Calvary so you might be delivered, yes, rescued, from your body of death. Hallelujah!

Excerpts From a Dead Man's Diary

We'll talk more about this in later chapters. For now, here are these poems, printed with the permission of the author. No names are mentioned; I don't want to destroy the *hope* that the other family members involved will see the fault, repent, and mend the broken relationships. I only reveal these past and "hidden secrets of the heart" of a very wonderful young man so you who are still entombed in the death of this Lazarus Generation might receive *hope*. These words are the cry of desperation and deep despair from the drowning millions. My friend wrote these poems as a young boy looking for answers. Thanks be to God and Father of our Lord Jesus; He gave him the answers in His own Son, Jesus.

To Die for You

Life is not long, and oh, to
die for you, what ecstasy.
Such a sweet pain, I'd do
it again and again.

Insatiable hunger, satisfactorily slow,
I see the edge cut deeper and oh,
to die for you...

The light's put out, but flames
burn still inside my soul,
a love for you.

The pain it grows, please make
it end, but oh, to die for you...
I would bear it again and again.

The Lazarus Generation

No tears from my eyes,
only blood from my lips.
For you I am silent…
through exquisite tortures.

My brain, it's melting, I hear
strange voices…
But oh, to die for you
still makes perfect sense.

Save me from trapping myself
in my dreams…
as questions of infinity cover me
in a web of fear.

I know my soul bleeds to
death as I stumble in endless night.
And I wonder why, I wonder how…
can I play with madness and die
for you?

Floating Thoughts

The blood trickles
down,
my heart, it breaks
you don't understand,
but who does?

Why? Why must it hurt?
Why can't I
cry?
I feel awful inside,
you hurt me.

Excerpts From a Dead Man's Diary

I, I love you still, and always will
although you don't love me…
like I do
you.

I wish you would talk…
it won't be that hard.
Tell me how you feel
but you can't
so…

I must go on, why…
there's no song
of love in my heart,
just pieces.

Each one screams
unheard
all through the night
repeating the cry
within me.

I need to move on,
stop
thinking these things, but I just can't
help it,
so I won't.

I wish I knew how to end,
this pain,
it seems to go on without any
end
in sight.

The Lazarus Generation

Why don't
people understand each other when they
all need someone
to be
with them?
I wish I could swiftly cease
to be
this me
the way that I am, but
who cares?

I'm trying
again, to figure it out,
to get over
her,
but I won't!

Maybe I'll give in
go quietly my
way,
you know where
it is,
eternal hell…

God,
why can't you see,
seems so
unfair,
don't want to go on…
part of this.

Guess I
have no choice,

Excerpts From a Dead Man's Diary

just wasn't asked
if I wouldn't mind
playing along.

I wish I had
died,
silent at birth
peace in my mind and soul
forever.

Now, turmoil and
pain…confusion and
questions, that none can answer
quite right.

So, I struggle on,
things might get
better
you never know…
I hope so.

Fallen

When the last star has fallen and there
is no light in the sky,
When death's sweet, chilling caress
is all we seek often,
When those we care most about
can only be hurt by futile
attempts to compensate
for ignorance,
When the hurt others feel cannot be
soothed by deaf ears, full of the

crashing of unsurpassable waves,
When love has been cheated so often
there is nothing left to give,
When faith is false, and the rumors
running through your head
are so blasphemous,
When questions ever surpass feeble
answers,
When words are empty, and there's
nothing left to say,
When clouds come as a blanket to
cover you in their impenetrable
darkness,
When their solace is more desirable
than the confines of this life,
When the precious delicate sounds of
thunder swiftly fade away,
When the beating of your heart resounds
as the discordant tolling of
blackened bells slowly swaying
in the sharp midnight air,
When the rays of the dawning sun have
paled beside the fires of
confusion burning within,
When the chains so carefully formed
become so obviously unbreakable,
When emotion is finally hidden in
perfect silence,
When all this and more has repeated
itself, the marked path

Excerpts From a Dead Man's Diary

winding its way through you forever,
When the wall has surrounded you and
insanity is so difficultly
denied,
When madness beckons, and it is clear
with what ease it could be overtaken,
When you've been through it all, and
there's no where else to go.
When the blade pleads for the sweet
taste of blood.
When lead seeks to press on urgently
through scarred memories, hideous
present, and unimaginable future,
When life's monotony and pain become
a toilsome burden no longer
bearable...
Why go on?

Sweet Insanity

Insanity, how seductively I can hear
you calling me.
Your face, as white as the pale
moonlight,
Hair, the pitch black of my soul,
Lips, as red as the life flowing
from my veins,
Eyes, as deep as the abyss from
which I seek to escape,
they reflect emotions I struggle
to hide.

The Lazarus Generation

In you I shall confide, for I can
hear you calling me.
I desperately need to feel your arms
about me, for you can see how
close I am to falling from this
wall, a precarious balance on
the precipice of logic.
Logic which so tightly binds me
to this world.

Wait, I have come...your sultry
whispering has drawn me.

Insanity, she embraces me, and we
sail out on clouded seas.
On past stars, yes they are ours,
sailing to infinity.
I come, oh sweet insanity, I can
hear you calling me!
Sweet insanity!

Games

It's all a game, and we all must play,
not over 'til it's over, can't wait
for that day.

I play with my mind, games in my
head, some are so cruel, I wish
I were dead.

I play with emotions, but I couldn't
start, to show you the pain,
in my broken heart.

Excerpts From a Dead Man's Diary

I'm in this with you, and you
are with me, regardless if that's
the way it should be.

I know I'm a dreamer, prob'ly a fool,
perhaps also blindly, another's tool.

There are no winners, this you should
know, inside frustrations continue
to grow.

Some choose to give up, get out of
this game, but there's no escape,
it's always the same.

Yes, it's all a game, we are just
players, running in circles,
up and down stairs.

I can't find the answers, this
game is a riddle. I'm going
to scream, I'm caught in the
middle.

Some say "Dear Jesus, he is your
friend." Because of this Jesus,
the game will not end!

Misunderstood

Mother, can't you see, this madness comes
again.
Father, don't you know, I'm tempted to
use this delicate blade.
Sister, you don't understand, or fully
realize my confusion.

The Lazarus Generation

Brother, please don't fantasize, of a fate
as real as mine.

I guess there's not much left to say,
that hasn't been repeated before,
and I guess we know what actions
are left us, hopefully it can end
this war, this insanity, this chaos,
all that seems left of me.

I pray this existence of mine has served
some purpose…
that my struggles with insanity
and death have not all been in vain.

I hope that those who follow will not
follow in my footsteps…
they only lead to pain and
suffering, for self and others,
until the soothing end is finally come.

One Way Street

Please take my hand, I've lost my sight
in looking for a dream.
I see your stars but all is night
here in this silent scream.

So empty, so lost, so out of place,
look for a one-way street.
Hold me Lord, finish this race,
I can't stand upon my feet.

Those eyes, so filled with pain and sorrow,
please show me holy light,

Excerpts From a Dead Man's Diary

And guard my vision until tomorrow,
my gift of second sight.

Don't let the tears and cries of others
turn your heart to stone.
In fear and confusion we are brothers,
no one walks alone.

Confide in me, your hurts and weeping,
I hear every single plea.
I give to you my peaceful sleeping,
I died upon that tree.

Anticipation

Sitting here, waiting, trembling
inside.
The words won't come, just can't get
them out!

I can feel my heart pounding within,
but it's not getting any easier.

To etch on this perfect blankness
the pain and emotion tearing
at me.

Come on! Get out! Please let me rid myself of this,
this part of me that hurts
beyond knowing.

I want to scream, but there is
no sound, I want to cry,
but the tears, I can't
let them fall now.

Sometimes I want to die, but…
that's too easy.

Dad, I Hated It (and You) When:

You left my brother and sister and me all alone when I was four.

When we were moving to another city in our State and you said Mom had better worry when you stop looking.

The many times you refused to listen to my brother and made him cry.

You hit my brother.

You accused my brother and/or me of sneaking out this summer.

You would preach on love and patience and tithing but I could find no example IN YOU.

We moved here and you never seemed to care that I took care of my brother and sister all day. You just wanted dinner.

You bragged about us kids and distorted the truth or didn't realize you had nothing to do with these accomplishments.

You forgot Mother's Day and her birthday.

I used to ask you for help to fix my bike and you'd say, "Go look at the manual." I don't want a manual for a father and I didn't understand it anyway.

You always bring home junk to put outside or in the kitchen.

You rarely complete a "project" (i.e. my car only took six months).

Excerpts From a Dead Man's Diary

Peaceful Sleeping

Oh please don't cry. O please don't weep,
For when I die, oh peaceful sleep.
I see your face, I see your tears,
So out of place, your hidden fears.
Undying love, I feel for you,
Infinite love, forever true.
A final kiss, a last goodbye,
I won't be missed, so please don't cry.
Don't feel so sad, for me it's night,
Try to be glad, for this is right.

Peaceful sleeping, a final end,
Always dreaming, the dying trend.
Peaceful sleeping, a cold dark mask,
I'm understanding my final task,
Peaceful sleeping, a dying trend,
Peaceful sleeping, the final end.

I wrote this about four months after I asked _____ out. I don't know why I wrote it. I just had to. It's not like I was really depressed....

"Dad, I hated it (and you) when...you would preach on love and patience and tithing but I could find no example in you...You forgot Mother's Day and her birthday...I used to ask you for help...I don't want a manual for a father...You always bring home junk...You rarely complete a project."

"Peaceful sleeping, a final end, always dreaming, the dying trend.... I wrote this about five months after I asked _____ out. I don't know why I wrote it. I just had to. It's not like I was really depressed...."

He may not have been depressed, but I was! I had never heard anything like this. Was this the pen of an "insane" boy, just a mixed-up kid? Was he a rarity in our society, a freak genetic break?

No! A million times, no! He is not an insane freak of genetics. He is a preacher's kid! He is a P.K. right here in middle-class America—the country of baseball, Chevrolet, and apple pie! We have produced a Lazarus Generation right in our "pastoral parsonage"!

Chapter 5

Prodigal Preachers Produce Prodigal Parsonages and P.K.'s

Why are preachers' kids and missionaries' kids some of the worst cases in the world? I believe I have some answers to this very important question. In this chapter I have a strong word for pastors, preachers, priests, and bishops—"whatever" people in church leadership call themselves.

"Wait a minute, Pastor! Who are you to tell us what to do?"

You just said it. I am a pastor and I have two daughters, 27 and 32 years old, who were raised in a preacher's home. My wife was raised in the home of her grandfather, a Pentecostal preacher, and his father was a preacher too! I had a great, great-uncle whose name was Ike Smith. He was an "old time" Methodist circuit-riding preacher. (Here's an interesting story: At the age of 107, Uncle Ike said he had one more sermon to preach before he died. He went to church that morning, preached his sermon, went home, ate lunch, sat down in a chair for a little nap, and then went home to be with Jesus!) As for myself, I preached my first sermon at the age of 13 and am now 52. My wife, Nancy, and I are both fourth-generation churchgoers, and we have produced fifth- and sixth-generation churchgoers. So I think I qualify to say what I need to say.

"Why would you be so bold, Preacher, to take such a strong approach to the issues of the pastor's parsonage?"

The reason is simple: a lot of the world's problems stem from the pastor's parsonage. Just look at current situations in the Church. I'm not writing this out of spite, but out of an honest desire to help pastors. I am one of them, and speaking for myself, I would want others to help me if they saw something that would kill me if I didn't stop it. Now, I'm not even close to being perfect! But after having gone through an overhaul by the Holy Ghost for the past few years,

Prodigal Preachers Produce Prodigal Parsonages and P.K.'s

I feel so much better that I would like to share my freedom with you too! It would be totally selfish and wrong for me not to share the new freedom I have found in Jesus.

A lot of good people would attend church, worship God, and give to God except for one thing: They see so much garbage in the pastor's parsonage that they refuse to draw near to God. They are afraid they will become like their preacher! What a sad saga for the Western minister: he has failed to win the lost of his own household and neighborhood because he failed to win in the wilderness of temptation!

Some time ago I learned that a highly visible preacher had been caught, by his son, with a woman other than his wife. As the disheartening news came, I thought, "This can't be, Lord!" I know this man well and had been in his evangelistic services in the past. I had heard his wonderful voice many times. I had seen his tears on Christian TV, seemingly for the lost, but perhaps it was because of a trapped mind and body that he cried. I'm sure many a pastor (like myself) was almost *envious* of such exposure on a prestigious program, wondering how we could share worldwide our vision and burden for the lost as he did.

Now look at the pain and at the bleeding hearts. Ask yourself, preacher, "Was it worth it?" All those years of ministry? All those years of saving the lost? All those years with a dear wife who stayed with you through literal hell on earth, fighting alongside you in the good and bad times? Is it worth it, my dear brother? I didn't think so!

"What should we do?"

Do what Jesus said: "Come unto Me, all ye that labour and are heavy laden, and I will give you rest" (Mt. 11:28 KJV).

It's time to return to fellowship with the Father and to stop fellowshipping with politicking preachers! If you would do that, then you wouldn't worry so much about your position and pocketbook! I know all about those district or national councils or conventions where you play the religious political games! You beg for revivals, or call old friends and buddies till you run out of them. You preach the same "blue ribbon" sermons you've preached at every revival service since Lord knows when! Do you want to know why those sermons went so well the first time? You had gotten them on your knees in fervent prayer and not out of some silly sermon book that gives three points and a conclusion!

Repent, my fellow laborers! Rededicate yourselves to the harvest—to the Lord of the harvest. Let's get our act together, preachers. Then our parsonages will once again be a place of peace and refuge from the world that we work and live in. Then even more importantly, we might just get our prodigal children (products of a Lazarus syndrome) back from sin! You

Prodigal Preachers Produce Prodigal Parsonages and P.K.'s

might welcome back that son or daughter who hated church, and you, because they heard you preach it but didn't see you live it at home!

God is at work in the preachers, parsonages, and prodigal preachers' kids and missionaries' kids. Then He will be able to work in the pews! Here is a final word from the Word of God:

Here is a trustworthy saying: If anyone sets his heart on being an overseer, he desires a noble task. Now the overseer must be above reproach, the husband of but one wife, temperate, self-controlled, respectable, hospitable, able to teach, not given to drunkenness, not violent but gentle, not quarrelsome, not a lover of money. He must manage his own family well and see that his children obey him with proper respect. (If anyone does not know how to manage his own family, how can he take care of God's church?) He must not be a recent convert, or he may become conceited and fall under the same judgment as the devil. He must also have a good reputation with outsiders, so that he will not fall into disgrace and into the devil's trap. Deacons, likewise, are to be men worthy of respect, sincere, not indulging in much wine, and not pursuing dishonest gain. They must keep hold of the deep truths of the faith with a clear conscience. They must first be tested; and then if there is nothing against them, let them serve as deacons. In the same way, their wives are to be women worthy of respect, not malicious talkers but temperate and trustworthy in everything. A deacon must be the husband of but one wife and must manage his children and his household well. Those who have served well gain an excellent standing and great assurance in their faith in Christ Jesus. Although I hope to come to you soon, I am writing you these instructions so that, if I am delayed, you will know how people ought to conduct themselves in God's household, which is the church of the living God, the pillar and foundation of the truth (1 Timothy 3:1-15).

Did you get that? Let me repeat verse 5: "If anyone does not know how to *manage* his own *family*, how can he take care of *God's church*?" It's not your church, it's God's. However, it is *your* family that you are responsible for. Take care of your family first, then God's church. I assure you that if you do so, you will never need to play religious politics again. God Himself will see to your needs and provide you with a place to preach and work till Jesus comes!

Chapter 6

The Prodigal Pew Pee-u!

Pigpen prodigals, produced by troubled preachers in unhealthy parsonages, are a major concern of our heavenly Father. They are so much His concern that one of the first fruits of this last-days revival will be the pastors' parsonages! Praise the Lord!

My point is, if it's going to change in the prodigal parsonage, it will also change in the prodigal pew (pee-u!). Pew warmers, you're next!

Let's look now at the parable of the lost son, "the Lazarus Generation," in Luke 15:11-32 and the parable of the vineyard and the two sons in Matthew 21:28-32.

Jesus continued: "There was a man who had two sons. The younger one said to his father, 'Father, give me my share of the estate.' So he divided his property between them. Not long after that, the younger son got together all he had, set off for a distant country and there squandered his wealth in wild living. After he had spent everything, there was a severe famine in that whole country, and he began to be in need. So he went and hired himself out to a citizen of that country, who sent him to his fields to feed pigs. He longed to fill his stomach with the pods that the pigs were eating, but no one gave him anything. When he came to his senses, he said, 'How many of my father's hired men have food to spare, and here I am starving to death! I will set out and go back to my father and say to him: Father, I have sinned against heaven and against you. I am no longer worthy to be called your son; make me like one of your hired men.' So he got up and went to his father. But while he was still a long way off, his father saw him and was filled with compassion for him; he ran to his son, threw his arms around him and kissed him. The son said to him, 'Father, I have sinned against heaven and against you. I am no longer worthy to be called your son.' But the father said to his servants, 'Quick! Bring the best robe and put it on him. Put a ring on his finger and sandals on his feet. Bring the fattened calf and kill it. Let's have a feast and celebrate. For this son of mine was dead and is alive again; he was lost and is found.' So they began to celebrate. Meanwhile, the older son was in the field. When he came near the house, he heard music and dancing. So he called one of the servants and asked him what was going on. 'Your brother has come,' he replied, 'and your father has killed the fattened calf because he has him back safe and sound.' The older brother became angry and refused to go in. So his father went out and pleaded with him. But he answered his father, 'Look! All these years I've been slaving for you and never disobeyed your orders. Yet you never gave me even a young goat so I could celebrate with my friends. But when this son of yours who has squandered your property with prostitutes comes home, you kill the fattened calf for him!' 'My son,' the father said, 'you are always with me, and everything I have is yours. But we had to celebrate and be glad, because this brother of yours was dead and is alive again; he was lost and is found' " (Luke 15:11-32).

"What do you think? There was a man who had two sons. He went to the first and said, 'Son, go and work today in the vineyard.' 'I will not,' he answered, but later he changed his mind and went. Then the father went to the other son and said the same thing. He answered, 'I will, sir,' but he did not go. Which of the two did what his father wanted?" "The first," they answered. Jesus said to them, "I tell you the truth, the tax collectors and the prostitutes are entering the kingdom of God ahead of

you. For John came to you to show you the way of righteousness, and you did not believe him, but the tax collectors and the prostitutes did. And even after you saw this, you did not repent and believe him" (Matthew 21:28-32).

These two parables are recorded so we might know *what* we are facing in this last-days generation and *how* to deal with it.

In the first parable there are three players: the father, the oldest son, and the younger son.

The father in the parable represents our heavenly Father, who is loving, kind, forgiving, merciful, gracious, and compassionate. He is ready to restore, any or all, this very hour!

The oldest son represents the legalist, the Pharisee, who until now has dominated our church world—be he ultra-conservative or ultra-liberal; charismatic or fundamental! He is the self-righteous, dyed-in-the wool, so-called "pillar" of the church (perhaps better known as an immovable object)! Pharisees have hindered others from receiving God's gracious forgiveness and caused trouble for Him by their own self-righteous and legalistic, holier-than-thou attitudes. They have kept others from rejoicing at God's mercy to those who would truly repent. (Our difficulty is in getting past all the "saints" in the pews who only judge, criticize, and put down those who, in their eyes, aren't "good enough" to get saved!)

Let us look at the contrast between our loving heavenly Father's response and the older son's reaction to the younger brother's return. The father was forgiving and overjoyed; the older brother was unforgiving and bitter. The father forgave because he was joyful. The older son refused to forgive because he was bitter.

The difference between bitterness and joy is our capacity to forgive. If you refuse to forgive people, you will miss the experience of true joy and of sharing that joy with them.

First Thessalonians 5:16 says, "Rejoice evermore" (KJV). Matthew 6:14 speaks about forgiveness. The key to rejoicing evermore is forgiveness! We must forgive the past, present, and future; hurts, offenses, and wounds from the brethren; religious pharisees, Dad, Mom, brothers, sisters, husbands, wives, and children; pastors, churches, denominations, and groups. That includes "organized religion," the proverbial "older brother," and everything that "he" represents!

The younger son represents this last-days generation, the Lazarus Generation. Let's look at this character. He is selfish, or self-centered. He shows a disregard for his father's authority as head of the family. He has no respect and no sense of responsibility. He is greedy and lusts for pleasure. He has a wild, rebellious spirit. All of these traits are typical of today's generation.

Second Timothy 3:1-5 and the Book of Jude provide greater descriptions of the older son and how we are to respond to him. He is a big hindrance to this last-days revival and harvest, but God is about to do something drastic about that!

> *But mark this: There will be terrible times in the last days. People will be lovers of themselves, lovers of money, boastful, proud, abusive, disobedient to their parents, ungrateful, unholy, without love, unforgiving, slanderous, without self-control, brutal, not lovers of the good, treacherous, rash, conceited, lovers of pleasure rather than lovers of God—having a form of godliness but denying its power...* (2 Timothy 3:1-5).

Godliness or *Godlessness*? The choice is ours. This reference in Second Timothy 3:1-5 describes our "righteous" generation. It's the "older brother" syndrome that God is beginning to separate from our midst as chaff from wheat!

> *Jesus told them another parable: "The kingdom of heaven is like a man who sowed good seed in his field. But while everyone was sleeping, his enemy came and sowed weeds among the wheat, and went away. When the wheat sprouted and formed heads, then the weeds also appeared. The owner's servants came to him and said, 'Sir, didn't you sow good seed in your field? Where then did the weeds come from?' 'An enemy did this,' he replied. The servants asked*

him, 'Do you want us to go and pull them up?' 'No,' he answered, 'because while you are pulling the weeds, you may root up the wheat with them. Let both grow together until the harvest. At that time I will tell the harvesters: First collect the weeds and tie them in bundles to be burned; then gather the wheat and bring it into my barn' " (Matthew 13:24-30).

Then He left the crowd and went into the house. His disciples came to Him and said, "Explain to us the parable of the weeds in the field." He answered, "The one who sowed the good seed is the Son of Man. The field is the world, and the good seed stands for the sons of the kingdom. The weeds are the sons of the evil one, and the enemy who sows them is the devil. The harvest is the end of the age, and the harvesters are angels. As the weeds are pulled up and burned in the fire, so it will be at the end of the age. The Son of Man will send out His angels, and they will weed out of His kingdom everything that causes sin and all who do evil. They will throw them into the fiery furnace, where there will be weeping and gnashing of teeth. Then the righteous will shine like the sun in the kingdom of their Father. He who has ears, let him hear (Matthew 13:36-43).

"Once again, the kingdom of heaven is like a net that was let down into the lake and caught all kinds of fish. When it was full, the fishermen pulled it up

on the shore. Then they sat down and collected the good fish in baskets, but threw the bad away. This is how it will be at the end of the age. The angels will come and separate the wicked from the righteous and throw them into the fiery furnace, where there will be weeping and gnashing of teeth. Have you understood all these things?" Jesus asked. "Yes," they replied. He said to them, "Therefore every teacher of the law who has been instructed about the kingdom of heaven is like the owner of a house who brings out of his storeroom new treasures as well as old" (Matthew 13:47-52).

In Luke 15:30 the older brother states, "But when this son of yours who has squandered your property...." The father replies, in verse 32, "But we had to celebrate and be glad, because this brother of yours was dead and is alive again; he was lost and is found." The Lazarus Generation was dead, lost, and without hope, but when Jesus, the *Resurrection*, appears on the scene and says, "Lazarus, come forth," he will! *That time is now!*

Chapter 7

I'm Glad I Was Not There...Let's Go!

And for your sake I am glad I was not there, so that you may believe. But let us go to him (John 11:15).

In previous chapters I talked about the *faith factor*. It is extremely important.

When Jesus told His disciples that Lazarus was "really" dead, it was the pivotal point in their faith factor. Would they now believe that Jesus could and would raise Lazarus from the dead? "*Now faith*" is required from this final generation as well. Jesus said, "I was glad for your sake that I was not there when

Lazarus died." Why? "So that you may believe. But let *us* go to him."

Jesus put them on the spot! It's *now faith*, not past or future faith. Those other faiths have been our generation's downfall.

"Oh yeah, Preacher. I believe that Jesus has healed and raised people from the dead. I also believe that He could do it again, if it was His will to do so. But I don't know about all that 'signs and wonders stuff!'"

Well, that "stuff" is the "stuff" that Jesus is made of and the "stuff" it will take to raise our Lazarus Generation from the dead!

Are we afraid to stand against the tide of so-called acceptable religious behavior and forms? Are we stuck with the status quo? Do we have only mainline religions and denominations that teach and live merely book-knowledge Christianity? Will we play it safe in our comfort-zone Christianity? Do we really believe that Jesus can pull off this resurrection? Or do we have a radical faith in the resurrected Savior and Lord? Do we dare follow the radical Christ? It's now or never!

So, what will it be: faith or fear? The choice is yours.

In summarizing the pivotal point of the whole matter, I give you this word. Read and hear very carefully the following call to persevere:

I'm Glad I Was Not There…Let's Go!

So do not throw away your confidence; it will be richly rewarded. You need to persevere so that when you have done the will of God, you will receive what He has promised. For in just a very little while, "He who is coming will come and will not delay. But My righteous one will live by faith. And if he shrinks back, I will not be pleased with him" (Hebrews 10:35-38).

Chapter 8

"Let *Us* Also Go!"

So then He told them plainly, "Lazarus is dead, and for your sake I am glad I was not there, so that you may believe. But let us go to him." Then Thomas (called Didymus) said to the rest of the disciples, "Let us also go, that we may die with Him" (John 11:14-16).

Jesus said it first; then Thomas said it. Praise the Lord! There is *hope*. Thomas got the "let us also go" part right. That's more than most ever do! At least he was committed to going with Jesus, was even willing to *die* with Him. God bless Thomas! "You may have been dubbed 'Doubting Thomas' by the many who read what you did after Jesus' resurrection, but Thomas, I take my hat off to you! You beat the rest of them to be the first to say, 'I'll go and I'll even die for You, Jesus.' "

So, what about the rest of the disciples? Well, I guess it worked so let's give Thomas an A+ for the *faith factor*!

Thomas also got the "die" part right. Spiritually speaking, though, it is death to self that Jesus desires from all of us! It requires total death to self to reach the gravesite of our Lazarus Generation.

We are not there yet; we must still face those "religious people" and their doctrines of doubt to even reach the tomb of Lazarus. Thus we must die to self before we can minister to the Lazarus people.

I have been crucified with Christ and I no longer live, but Christ lives in me. The life I live in the body, I live by faith in the Son of God, who loved me and gave Himself for me (Galatians 2:20).

Chapter 9

Jesus, Three; Lazarus, Four!

On His arrival, Jesus found that Lazarus had already been in the tomb for four days. Bethany was less than two miles from Jerusalem, and many Jews had come to Martha and Mary to comfort them in the loss of their brother (John 11:17-19).

Jesus waited for four days. Why? The Jews and religious groups believed and taught (and still do today) that a man's spirit hovered over his dead body for three days before it departed. Jesus' wait of three days was proof to every religion that He has the power to raise the truly dead!

However, Jesus was in His tomb for only three days, while Lazarus was in his tomb for four days. Why only three for Jesus and four for Lazarus? Look at the prophecy David made concerning Jesus. After you read it, you will see just how important it was for Jesus to be dead only three days and not four:

Lord, You have assigned me my portion and my cup; You have made my lot secure. The boundary lines have fallen for me in pleasant places; surely I have a delightful inheritance. I will praise the Lord, who counsels me; even at night my heart instructs me. I have set the Lord always before me. Because He is at my right hand, I will not be shaken. Therefore my heart is glad and my tongue rejoices; my body also will rest secure, because You will not abandon me to the grave, nor will You let Your Holy One see decay. You have made known to me the path of life; You will fill me with joy in Your presence, with eternal pleasures at Your right hand (Psalm 16:5-11).

Even Jesus had to have absolute trust in faith and total commitment to His Father's will. Oh, the faith of Jesus! The prophecy says, "...my body also will rest secure, because You will not *abandon me to the grave*, nor will You let Your Holy One [Jesus] see *decay*" (vv. 9-10).

If Jesus had seen decay, we would have had absolutely no *hope*! Our resurrection and Lazarus' would have been only a passing desire in the night of deep despair, in our "Titanic" ocean liner instead of a ship of Zion! But because He did not see decay, *we have hope*!

In John 11:17 we see that, by the time Jesus arrived, Lazarus had been in the tomb for four days. Then jumping ahead to verse 39, we hear Martha say a word about it:

…"by this time there is a bad odor, for he has been there four days."

"Four days" tells us that Lazarus must have been rotting in the grave! In other words, there was *absolutely no hope*! There was no reason to believe that any life was left in the man. However, there was a purpose behind it all!

Do you remember what the "religious skeptics" said about Jesus not really being raised from the dead? When He was reported to be alive after His resurrection they had their doubts about it! Let's look at Matthew's account of their reaction:

*The next day, the one after Preparation Day, the chief priests and the Pharisees went to Pilate. "Sir," they said, **"we remember that while He was still alive that deceiver said, 'After three days I will rise again.'** So give the order for the tomb to be made secure until the third day. Otherwise, His disciples may come and steal the body and tell the people that*

*He has been raised from the dead. This **last deception** will be worse than the first." "Take a guard," Pilate answered. "Go, make the tomb as secure as you know how." So they went and made the tomb secure by putting a seal on the stone and posting the guard* (Matthew 27:62-66).

Well, Jesus was smart! He gave *all* skeptics in all generations something to think about: a little *preview* of His resurrection. He was showing them, if they had doubts about His coming out of the grave, that He could raise a totally dead, actually rotting human being, as a small sample of the *resurrection power* that gives life to anyone or to all!

Are you convinced yet, you "religious skeptics" of our generation, who doubt almost anything and everything God has said would happen? You go to church, you pray, you read the Bible, yet you say, "There's *no hope* for Johnny, Sue, Bill, Joe, Mary...Lazarus! We have *no hope* of seeing a change in the condition of our generation."

The governments of the world's system are, for the most part, very religious, but they too have given up hope. School systems struggle for new ideas— New Age ideas. They are forever changing programs to try to help the kids! Hospitals work day and night, seemingly without end. They build bigger and better barns to hold the psychotic, ill, dying, and diseased, but they cannot find a cure for AIDS! Even with all of our money, it seems there is no hope for the rotting flesh of multiplied millions worldwide who are either dying or suffering from malnutrition or diseases without treatment.

Where is the Church in all this mess? I mean the Body of Christ—the pure, lovely, powerful, bold, ready-for-Christ Church. Do you know where they are? "They?" you ask. Yes, "they" are divided.

They are not yet the "one Lord, one Body, one baptism, one God" Church of the Bible. Instead, they are in a bunch of different denominations, doctrines, and dogmas; they are diluted and demonized—donkeys' heads and doves' dung!

That's the good news! Now for the bad news. Keep in mind, though, that I'm not talking about Jesus and His true disciples. I'm talking about religion! I don't mean old-time religion, just "religion." If we still had old-time religion, then all this stuff wouldn't be a problem! We'd have all-night prayer meetings, not all-night videos and pizza parties and Bingo games! The Church needs to pray all night, not party all night! Is it any wonder people aren't saved on Sunday? Well-meaning pastors, preachers, teachers, and denominationalists have primarily chosen the *comforting* ministry, not the *deliverance* ministry!

We may not like it, but we must soon make a choice! You see, this Lazarus Generation will require *deliverance*,

The Lazarus Generation

not comforting! You can't comfort a dead man or his family. AIDS patients and their families want answers, not pity. They want a cure, not comfort.

In Lazarus' situation, Jesus came to deliver. The Jews came to comfort Mary and Martha. There is a big difference. Unfortunately, we've spent millions on comfort ministries—on counselling couches and coffee tables. But honestly, once those ministries discover that the person has a problem, they could do absolutely nothing. That is, they couldn't do anything unless they were one of those "weird preacher creatures" who believe in the deliverance ministry and not the normal comfort ministry!

Have you forgotten that the Church is a hospital for the sick and dying; that it's for the sinners and not just for the saints? In a hospital you don't have only a delivery room to deliver babies. You also have a deliverance room to cut out sickness, pain, demons, depression, fears, death, the past, failures, etc.! The Church of Jesus Christ is not a finishing school for the very religious, but a general hospital. We treat everyone and everything! Our Lazarus Generation shall be raised up to be ready to meet Jesus when He comes! That will happen as we change our ministry from a comfort zone to a portable hospital that goes to the battlefield, where the real war is being fought—*in our streets.*

So, pastors, churches, deacons—let's get out of our "ivory palaces" and don our armor for Christ

Jesus, Three; Lazarus, Four!

Jesus! We have the Holy Ghost, the Father, His angels, their power (which is our power), prayer, the Word, the blood of Jesus, and His name to go into all the world and preach the gospel of deliverance. That is exactly what this gospel is all about: deliverance. It is the truth, and when you know the truth, it will set you (and this Lazarus Generation) totally free!

Before I close this chapter, let me remind you of what the Holy Spirit says to the so-called, hopeless Lazarus Generation: "The AIDS *factor* will be totally eradicated through the *faith factor* in and by the *Jesus factor*, who is the *resurrection factor*!" *Oh, what hope*! Get ready, Lazarus, here comes Jesus to raise you from the dead!

Chapter 10

Look Who's Pouting Now!

*When Martha heard that Jesus was coming, she went out to meet Him, **but Mary stayed at home*** (John 11:20).

The King James Version of John 11:20 states, "...but Mary sat still in the house." *Strong's Concordance* indicates that the root of the word for "sat" means "immovable."[1] I also looked up the definition of *pouting*

---

1. James Strong, *The Exhaustive Concordance of the Bible*, Peabody, MA: Hendrickson Publishers, n.d.

and found it to mean exactly the point I want to make in this chapter. Webster says, "pout *n* (1591) **1**: a protrusion of the lips expressive of displeasure **2** *pl*: a fit of pique."[2] What does "pique" mean? Here is what *Webster's Ninth New Collegiate Dictionary* said: "pique *n* (1592): a transient feeling of wounded vanity : a fit of resentment." "Piqued" is the same as "wounded pride!" Pride got the devil and it will surely get you too!

Whose pride has been wounded here? Look at sweet "religious" Mary. "When Martha heard that Jesus was coming, she went out to meet Him" (Jn. 11:20). Let's stop here for a moment. Do you realize that you need to be ready to go out to meet Him when He comes, both now (spiritually) in this revival, restoration, or harvest time and (literally) when He comes back for His Church, the Bride of Christ? Consider these passages:

> *According to the Lord's own word, we tell you that we who are still alive, who are left till the coming of the Lord, will certainly not precede those who have fallen asleep. For the Lord Himself will come down from heaven, with a loud command, with the voice of the archangel and with the trumpet call of God, and the dead in Christ will rise first. After that, we who are still alive and are left will be caught up together with them in the clouds to meet the Lord in*

---

2. *Webster's Ninth New Collegiate Dictionary*, Springfield, MA: Merriam-Webster Inc., 1988.

the air. And so we will be with the Lord forever. Therefore encourage each other with these words (1 Thessalonians 4:15-18).

...For the trumpet will sound, the dead will be raised imperishable, and we will be changed. For the perishable must clothe itself with the imperishable, and the mortal with immorality. When the perishable has been clothed with the imperishable, and the mortal with immortality, then the saying that is written will come true: "Death has been swallowed in victory. Where, O death, is your victory? Where, O death, is your sting?" The sting of death is sin, and the power of sin is the law. But thanks be to God! He gives us the victory through our Lord Jesus Christ. Therefore, my dear brothers, stand firm. Let nothing move you. Always give yourselves fully to the work of the Lord, because you know that your labor in the Lord is not in vain (1 Corinthians 15:52-58).

So you can either *pout* or *shout*. The choice is yours.

John 11:20 continues, "But Mary stayed at home."

"If that's the kind of services they are having, then I'll just stay home! All of that shouting, dancing, and whooping; those victory marches [glorified Jericho marches]; people falling out in the Holy Ghost, speaking in tongues, prophesying, preaching, praying—powerful, pulsating! I'll just stay home! They are just too radical for me—I like it quiet!"

Unfortunately, that is deathly (deadly) quiet—like a dark, damp dungeon of doom and death type of church service. You may possibly be attending one. There's death in the pulpit and death in the pew! Martha said, "But, Lord, by this time there is a bad odor, for he has been there four days" (see Jn. 11:39). Does your church have a bad odor? Has it been dead four (no, *for*) *years*? And you, like Mary, wanted to stay home for that? Isn't that pride?

"Mary, Mary, quite contrary," how does your church grow? Well, it doesn't grow at all. It's dead, and has a really bad odor. Only "alive and well" churches produce life!

Oh, by the way, about those flowers that you grow in your garden—take a few to your church next Sunday. Why next Sunday? Well, because it's probably closed till then. Most churches are closed during the week, or might as well be! "Oh, it's only a Bible study, or an old 'prayer meeting,' so I'll just stay *home!*" By the way, those flowers are graveside bouquets (a pun is intended)!

Consider this, those of you who are like Mary:

Let us not give up meeting together, as some are in the habit of doing, but let us encourage one another—and all the more as you see the Day approaching (Hebrews 10:25).

Look Who's Pouting Now!

Do you want to stay home and pout? I didn't think so! Mary didn't either. Martha, in John 11:28, went back and called her sister, Mary, aside. " 'The Teacher is here,' she said, 'and is asking for you.' " When contrary Mary heard that, she quickly got up and went to Jesus.

There is *hope* for all the Marys who pouted in their prideful pew! There is *hope* because of "all the commotion" at Goshen.

> *Now Jacob sent Judah ahead of him to Joseph to get directions to Goshen. When they arrived in the region of Goshen, Joseph had his chariot made ready and went to Goshen to meet his father Israel. As soon as Joseph appeared before him, he threw his arms around his father and wept for a long time. Israel said to Joseph, "Now I am ready to die, since I have seen for myself that you are still alive." Then Joseph said to his brothers and to his father's household, "I will go up and speak to Pharaoh and will say to him, 'My brothers and my father's household, who were living in the land of Canaan, have come to me. The men are shepherds; they tend livestock, and they have brought along their flocks and herds and everything they own.' When Pharaoh calls you in and asks, 'What is your occupation?' you should answer, 'Your servants have tended livestock from our boyhood on, just as our fathers did.' Then you will be allowed to settle in the region of*

Goshen, for all shepherds [true shepherds] *are detestable to the Egyptians* [hirelings in our religious world]." *Joseph went and told Pharaoh, "My father and brothers, with their flocks and herds and everything they own, have come **from the land of Canaan and are now in Goshen**." He chose five of his brothers and presented them before Pharaoh. Pharaoh asked the brothers, "What is your occupation?" "Your servants are shepherds," they replied to Pharaoh, "just as our fathers were." They also said to him, "We have come to live here awhile, **because the famine is severe in Canaan and your servants' flocks have no pasture. So now, please let your servants settle in Goshen**." Pharaoh said to Joseph, "Your father and your brothers have come to you"* (Genesis 46:28–47:5).

(Goshen was an oasis of great blessing in Egypt's famine.)

Mary, you haven't seen anything yet! All the commotion at Goshen is nothing compared to what's coming: the resurrection of this Lazarus Generation—*hopefully* in your church! Even bigger than that is the time Jesus will say, "Come forth!" Don't miss it!

He won't just say, "Lazarus, be comforted," but "Lazarus, come forth!" Do you see the difference? It won't be comfort-able Christianity, but come-forth Christianity! So change your minds. Don't stay at home;

come to where all the commotion at Goshen is going on! There will be real revival and green pastures (good food and preaching), for all those starving sheep. Jesus said it: "Feed My lambs, My sheep, and tend My flocks" (see Jn. 21:15-17). If today's pastors (shepherds) don't tend the sheep, God will raise up His true shepherds to feed and tend those sheep! Consider your own position; then choose wisely—and quickly!

There are churches, and true shepherds pastoring those churches, that are on fire, in revival fellowships. These are the places that God is raising up to minister to this Lazarus Generation. These churches are nontraditional, nonconforming, nonreligious, noncompromising, and radical! No one can deny the life, power, and witness of these different and radical groups!

Chapter 11

Look Who's Believing Now!

"Lord," Martha said to Jesus, "if You had been here, my brother would not have died. But I know that even now God will give You whatever You ask." Jesus said to her, "Your brother will rise again." Martha answered, "I know he will rise again in the resurrection at the last day." Jesus said to her, "I am the resurrection and the life. He who believes in Me will live, even though he dies; and whoever lives and believes in Me will never die. Do you believe this?" "Yes, Lord," she told Him, "I believe that You are the Christ, the Son of God, who was to come into the *world." ... When Mary reached the place where Jesus was and saw Him, she fell at His feet and said, "Lord, if You had been here, my brother would not have died"* (John 11:21-27,32).

The key word is *believe*. Jesus said to her, "He who believes in Me...Do you believe this?" "Yes, Lord! I believe! I believe that You're not just the Savior in the *future tense*, but also in the *present tense*. I believe that You are the Christ now, the Son of God, who was to come into the world—yes, into my world of unbelief, fear, and doubt, to give me *hope* of a 'better' resurrection!"

And what more shall I say? I do not have time to tell about Gideon, Barak, Samson, Jephthah, David, Samuel and the prophets, who through faith conquered kingdoms, administered justice, and gained what was promised; who shut the mouths of lions, quenched the fury of the flames, and escaped the edge of the sword; whose weakness was turned to strength; and who became powerful in battle and routed foreign armies. Women received back their dead, raised to life again. Others were tortured and refused to be released, so that they might gain a better resurrection. Some faced jeers and flogging, while still others were chained and put in prison. They were stoned; they were sawed in two; they were put to death by the sword. They went about in sheepskins and goatskins, destitute, persecuted and mistreated—the world was not worthy of them.

Look Who's Believing Now!

They wandered in deserts and mountains, and in caves and holes in the ground. These were all commended for their faith, yet none of them received what had been promised. God had planned something better for us so that only together with us would they be made perfect (Hebrews 11:32-40).

Let's look up, not down! This "better" resurrection is very near!

In John 11:31 we read that when the Jews who had been with Mary in the house noticed how quickly she got up and went out, they followed her, supposing she was going to the tomb to mourn.

Therefore this speaks to the Jew also. I mean the real, natural born, living in Canaan land, Jew. The Israelites also need to get this picture! That "Gentile Jesus" is the Messiah— as their *own* race put it. Martha and Mary, who are Jews, said it: "I believe that You are the Christ [Messiah], the Son of God, who was to come into the world" (Jn. 11:27). Today's modern Jew will soon take notice, as did those Jews who followed Mary. It does no good to call Martha and Mary "Gentile believers" just because they believed in the "Gentile Jesus." My dear seed of Abraham, you are about to see one of the greatest revivals among the Gentiles that this world will ever see— and it will shock your "Holy Land" socks off!

Mary and Martha are not attending the graveside service of a dying or dead "Gentile Jesus" religion!

No; we are not into religion but into *resurrection*. You simply supposed that Gentile Mary was still pouting in her religious pride. Instead she's getting in a hurry for a different reason.

Jesus, the true Messiah, is coming to raise up a Jesus-believing Church who *is* the Bride of *our* Messiah! Jesus is Lord of both Jew and Gentile. He raised their Lazarus and He will raise our Lazarus. Get ready! We will be attending a resurrection service for the dead Gentile Lazarus.

Many of you are already getting reports of revival (not just survival) in many nations of the world. There are reports from China, Russia, Africa, Latin America (where 400 people every hour come to know Jesus), Europe, and even the U.S.A. We are your friends, dear Israelites. So not only take the "Patriot Missiles," but also take this "Missile of Love" from a concerned patriot! A prodding, provoking, Protestant, Pentecostal pastor, loves the Jew. When you love, you won't need more Patriot missiles. Learn from Saul of Tarsus:

And Saul was there, giving approval to his death. On that day a great persecution broke out against the church at Jerusalem, and all except the apostles were scattered throughout Judea and Samaria. Godly men buried Stephen and mourned deeply for him. But Saul began to destroy the church. Going from house to house, he dragged off men and women and put them in prison. Those who had been scattered preached the word wherever they went. Philip went down to a city in Samaria and proclaimed the Christ there. When the crowds heard Philip and saw the miraculous signs he did, they all paid close attention to what he said. With shrieks, evil spirits came out of many, and many paralytics and cripples were healed. So there was great joy in that city (Acts 8:1-8).

Meanwhile, Saul was still breathing out murderous threats against the Lord's disciples. He went to the high priest and asked him for letters to the synagogues in Damascus, so that if he found any there who belonged to the Way, whether men or women, he might take them as prisoners to Jerusalem. As he neared Damascus on his journey, suddenly a light from Heaven flashed around him. He fell to the ground and heard a voice say to him, "Saul, Saul, why do you persecute Me?" "Who are You, Lord?" Saul asked. "I am Jesus, whom you are persecuting," he replied. "Now get up and go into the city, and you will be told what you must do" (Acts 9:1-6).

Please learn from Saul (Paul). He couldn't kill this Gentile, Jesus-believing Way! So what did he do? He joined them! "If you can't lick 'em, join 'em!" Consider wisely, my brother. I love you, seed of our father Abraham.

Chapter 12

Jesus Is Lord!

"Lord," Martha said to Jesus, "if You had been here, my brother would not have died. But I know that even now God will give You whatever You ask" (John 11:21-22).

That was a negative statement, but it was true. Lazarus would not have died, for Jesus *is* Lord over all sickness and disease, the spirit of death and Hades, and the spirits of infirmities! Jesus said, "All power is given unto Me in heaven [there's no sickness there] and in earth [there's lots of sickness and death here] (Mt. 28:18 KJV).

John 11:22 says, "But I know that even now…." That's four days dead. Sound familiar to anyone?

> *...for I know whom I have believed, and am persuaded that He [Jesus] is able to keep that which I have committed unto Him against that day* (2 Timothy 1:12 KJV).

I know that even now God Jehovah, the Father of Abraham, will (and it is His will) raise this Lazarus Generation. Moreover, Jesus said to you and me, "Ask the Father anything in My name, [the name of Jesus] and I [Jesus] will do it for you" (see Jn. 14:13; 15:16; 16:23).

"So I ask now, Lord Jesus, in Your name. Father God, hear my prayer and raise this Lazarus Generation from the dead! For it is Your will!" Now I give you this great confidence and hope:

> *I write these things to you who believe in the name of the Son of God so that you may know that you have eternal life. This is the confidence we have in approaching God: that if we ask anything according to His will, He hears us. And if we know that He hears us—whatever we ask—we know that we have what we asked of Him. If anyone sees his brother commit a sin that does not lead to death, he should pray and God will give him life. I refer to those whose sin does not lead to death. There is a sin that leads to death. I am not saying that he should pray about that. All wrongdoing is sin, and there is sin that does not lead to death. We know that anyone born of God does not continue to sin; the one who was born of God keeps him safe, and the evil one*

cannot harm him. We know that we are children of God, and that the whole world is under the control of the evil one. We know also that the Son of God has come and has given us understanding, so that we may know Him who is true. And we are in Him who is true—even in His Son Jesus Christ. He is the true God and eternal life. Dear children, keep yourselves from idols (1 John 5:13-21).

The Father is still at work today. Just ask Him, in Jesus' name!

Chapter 13

The Resurrection Factor

Jesus said to her, "Your brother will rise again." Martha answered, "I know he will rise again in the resurrection at the last day." Jesus said to her, "I am the resurrection and the life. He who believes in Me will live, even though he dies; and whoever lives and believes in Me will never die. Do you believe this?" "Yes, Lord," she told Him, "I believe that You are the Christ, the Son of God, who was to come into the world." And after she had said this, she went back and called her sister Mary aside. "The Teacher is here," she said, "and is asking for you." When Mary heard this, she got up quickly and went to Him. Now Jesus had not yet entered the village, but was still at the place where Martha had met Him. When the Jews who had been with Mary in the house, comforting her, noticed how quickly she got up and went out, they followed her, supposing she was going to the tomb to mourn there. When Mary reached the place where Jesus was and saw Him, she fell at His feet and said, "Lord, if You had been here, my brother would not have died" (John 11:23-32).

This discussion will go quickly; be prepared to be awakened! I'm going to review some things from the previous chapters. Get ready to be shocked into reality!

"Jesus said to her, 'Your brother will rise again' " (Jn. 11:23). "I'm the resurrection" said that! Martha answered, "I know he will rise again [the faith factor] in the resurrection at the last day." That's good theology (prophecy). She spoke of more than the general resurrection of the dead in Christ at the resurrection in the last day, which is a literal day when Jesus comes. She spoke of that very day!

In John 11:25, Jesus said to Martha, "I am the resurrection and the life." In other words, He said, "Martha, I *am* the resurrection; I don't just have the power to raise the dead. I *am* life; I don't just have the power to restore it." Jesus also said to her, "He who believes in Me will live, even though he dies." There

He spoke of physical death and *literal physical resurrection*. Then He went on to say, "And whoever lives and believes in Me will never die. Do you believe this?" Whoever *lives in Him* and *believes in Him* will never die *spiritually*. Do *you* believe this?

Martha, you have passed the test on the resurrection! Martha had the right answer at verse 27: " 'Yes, Lord,' she told Him, 'I believe that You are the Christ, the Son of God, who was to come into the world.' " That's what Paul preached also:

But what does it say? "The word is near you; it is in your mouth and in your heart," that is, the word of faith we are proclaiming: That if you confess with your mouth, "Jesus is Lord," and believe in your heart that God raised Him from the dead, you will be saved. For it is with your heart that you believe and are justified, and it is with your mouth that you confess and are saved (Romans 10:8-10).

Mary, where are you? Are you still pouting? Martha called her sister aside and said, "The Teacher is here" (Jn. 11:28). Listen to the Teacher! He has just taught the lesson on who He is and was and what He is about to do. Martha continued, "And [He] is asking for you" (Jn. 11:28). It doesn't matter if you are mad at me, dear pew-sitter. I love you, so please quit pouting.

Jesus is asking for you too!

"When Mary heard this, she got up quickly and went to Him" (Jn. 11:29). You too, quickly, believe that Jesus loves you in spite of your hurt feelings. You're hurt because you don't understand who He really is: the *resurrection* and the *life*. It's okay! Just go out to *Him* as Mary did. Jesus requires us to come to Him! "Come unto Me, all ye that labour and are heavy laden [labor, trials], and I will give you rest" (Mt. 11:28 KJV).

When the Jews saw Mary leave quickly, they followed her, supposing she was going out to the tomb to mourn there (see Jn. 11:31). All that the religious think is "I suppose." Suppose means "to the tomb to mourn"!

In verse 32, Mary is in the same situation Martha was in earlier: "Lord, if You...." It's not bad theology, but it's incomplete! Are you in this same situation?

Chapter 14

They Wept; He Wept!

When Jesus saw her weeping, and the Jews who had come along with her also weeping, He was deeply moved in spirit and troubled. "Where have you laid him?" He asked. "Come and see, Lord," they replied. Jesus wept. Then the Jews said, "See how He loved him!" But some of them said, "Could not He who opened the eyes of the blind man have kept this man from dying?" Jesus, once more deeply moved, came to the tomb. It was a cave with a stone laid across the entrance (John 11:33-38).

They wept; He wept. However, believe me, their weeping was for two totally different reasons! The Jews wept for their grief. Jesus wept for their unbelief! Belief or grief? The choice is yours.

Verse 33 says, "When Jesus saw her [Mary] weeping, and the Jews who had come along with her also weeping, He was deeply moved in spirit and troubled."

In Matthew 8:14-17 we find this:

When Jesus came into Peter's house, He saw Peter's mother-in-law lying in bed with a fever. He touched her hand and the fever left her, and she got up and began to wait on Him. When evening came, many who were demon-possessed were brought to Him, and He drove out the spirits with a word and healed all the sick. This was to fulfill what was spoken through the prophet Isaiah: "He took up our infirmities and carried our diseases" (Matthew 8:14-17).

Romans 8:22-27 states:

*We know that the whole creation has been groaning as in the pains of childbirth right up to the present time. Not only so, but we ourselves, who have the firstfruits of the Spirit, **groan inwardly** as we wait eagerly for our adoption as sons, the redemption of our bodies. For in this hope we were saved. But hope that is seen is no hope at all. Who hopes for what he already has? But if we hope for what we do not yet have, we wait for it patiently. In the same way, the Spirit helps us in our weakness. We do not know what we ought to pray for, **but the Spirit Himself intercedes for us with groans that words cannot express. And He who searches our hearts knows the mind of the Spirit, because the Spirit***

They Wept; He Wept!

intercedes for the saints in accordance with God's will (Romans 8:22-27).

Jesus was deeply moved for both Mary and those Jews. He groaned in His spirit, for both were His own blood kin. Mary and the Jews who were there wept for grief, but the latter also *wept* in *unbelief*. That is the reason Jesus was troubled. He was deeply moved by compassion. Hebrews 4:15 says that Jesus is moved by "the feeling of our infirmities" (KJV). But Jesus was also troubled in His spirit because of their unbelief.

John 11:35 says that Jesus wept, and now we know why. It's the shortest verse in the Bible, but it speaks volumes! Is He deeply moved over you, or is He troubled over you? Verses 36-37 tell us again why He was troubled over the Jews. Unbelief causes Jesus real grief. The Jews said, "See how He loved him!" They were right, you know. If they could have just stopped there, they too would have seen His great love that they spoke of from their own mouths. They would have seen Him meet their real sorrow and grief too!

However, at this juncture some of them said, "Could not ['could not', never did anything] He who opened the eyes of the blind man have kept this man from dying?" (Jn. 11:37) Jesus could have and would have, but He told us back in verse 4 why, when He heard that Lazarus was sick, He didn't leave immediately but stayed where He was yet another two days. Jesus said, "This sickness will not end in death. No, it is for God's glory so that God's Son may be *glorified through it"* (Jn. 11:4). It was a *faith* declaration!

*But the angel said to them, "Do not be afraid. I bring you good news of great joy that will be for all the people. Today in the town of David a Savior has been born to you; He is Christ the Lord. This will be a sign to you: You will find a baby wrapped in cloths and lying in a manger." Suddenly a great company of the heavenly host appeared with the angel, praising God and saying, "**Glory to God in the highest, and on earth peace to men on whom His favor rests'** "* (Luke 2:10-14).

The revelation of Jesus Christ, which God gave Him to show His servants what must soon take place. He made it known by sending His angel to His servant John, who testifies to everything he saw—that is, the word of God and the testimony of Jesus Christ. Blessed is the one who reads the words of this prophecy, and blessed are those who hear it and take to heart what is written in it, because the time is near. John, To the seven churches in the province of Asia: Grace and peace to you from Him who is, and who was, and who is to come, and from the seven spirits before His throne, and from Jesus Christ, who is the faithful witness, the firstborn from the dead, and the ruler of the kings of the earth. To Him who loves us and has freed us from our sins by His blood, and has made us to be a kingdom and priests to serve His God and Father—to Him be glory and power for ever and ever! Amen. Look, He is coming with the clouds, and every eye will see Him, even those who pierced Him; and all the peoples of the earth will mourn because of Him. So shall it be! Amen. "I am the Alpha and the Omega," says the Lord God, "who is, and who was, and who is to come, the Almighty" (Revelation 1:1-8).

Yes, God's own Son, Jesus, will be glorified! For He *always* glorifies His Father, who is in Heaven. The Son is about to receive such glory from His Father that the whole world won't be able to contain it!

Chapter 15

"Take Away the Stone!"

Jesus, once more deeply moved, came to the tomb. It was a cave with a stone laid across the entrance. "Take away the stone," He said. "But, Lord," said Martha, the sister of the dead man, "by this time there is a bad odor, for he has been there four days." ... So they took away the stone. Then Jesus looked up and said, "Father, I thank You that You have heard Me" (John 11:38-39,41).

Church, *we* must take away the stone from the opening of Lazarus' tomb. Jesus said so! It is not an option, but a command. He is our Commander-in-Chief. However, obeying such a command requires total commitment. It demands total trust, total faith and obedience, to raise the Lazarus Generation! It means total cooperation with Jesus, who is at the helm of Zion's ship. We need Jesus, and He needs our help, our co-efforts, to do this job. Therefore, we must do our part in this coalition to "free" Lazarus from his tomb.

So, remove the stone of doubt and fear, the stone of grief and unbelief! Roll away the largest stone of all: the stone of religion and religious people! "But Lord, by this time the man stinks!" There will be a bad odor, but don't let that keep you from raising the dead! Dead things are supposed to smell. All religion and unbelief stinks too!

Jesus had to deal with people like that as well. They were called "Sadducees." They were "Sad-you-see" because they didn't believe in the resurrection of the dead or in angels. Such people exist even today. They say, "Pray and seek, so you might just return in your next life as a bird, or better still, as a butterfly." (What garbage.) I have only one question. If you're a pretty little butterfly and a hungry bird comes near, whose lunch will you be in your next life?

So the stone of "religion" is a real nut to crack! Don't worry, though; we win! Read the last chapter

"Take Away the Stone!"

in the Bible. Revelation 22:20 says, "He who testifies to these things says, 'Yes, I am coming soon.' Amen. Come, Lord Jesus."

First though, Lazarus must be raised from the dead! If we, the Church, would have more prayer meetings and less stare meetings, we might just be able to get that stone rolled away! By "stare meetings" I mean the time we watch that television so much! We have red eyes, but it's not from weeping over the lost. It's from staring at the TV set and lingering too long at watching "the dregs of sin in the cesspools of society"! For instance, there is "As the Stomach Turns"; "As the World Twirls"; and "Where, Oh Where Are My Kids?" Unfortunately, some of them are drunk, drugged, depressed, and diseased. One was even caught eating human flesh! We are truly experiencing a repeat of the besieged city of Samaria.

The king replied, "If the Lord does not help you, where can I get help for you? From the threshing floor? From the winepress?" Then he asked her, "What's the matter?" She answered, "This woman said to me, 'Give up your son so we may eat him today, and tomorrow we'll eat my son.' So we cooked by son and ate him. The next day I said to her, 'Give up your son so we may eat him,' but she had hidden him." When the king heard the woman's words, he tore his robes. As he went along the wall, the people looked, and there, underneath, he had sackcloth on his body. He said, "May God deal with me, be it ever so severely, if the head of Elisha son of Shaphat remains on his shoulders today!" (2 Kings 6:27-31)

Are you ready to move the stone away? I am, so let's do it!

Chapter 16

He Came Out Alive—But Bound

When He had said this, Jesus called in a loud voice, "Lazarus, come out!" The dead man came out, his hands and feet wrapped with strips of linen, and a cloth around his face. Jesus said to them, "Take off the grave clothes and let him go" (John 11:43-44).

Jesus *called out* in a loud voice, "Lazarus, come out!" And he did. In spite of no faith, little faith, great faith, and the God-kind of faith—all of which were present—he came out! We can't let anything or anyone keep us from going with Jesus into all this world, which is *filled* with graves with Lazaruses in them. These graves have been made by religions, godless governments, sin, sickness, diseases, fears, rejection, abortion, rape, hate.... If you can name it, there is a tomb for it and you can be sure that there is a Lazarus in it!

But, hallelujah, Jesus and His disciples are coming on the scene with resurrection power! They are coming with faith to roll the stone away so Jesus can say to Lazarus, "Come out!" Come out of your hell holes, people! Come out of your depressions, fears, soul ties, and generational curses! Come out of your diseased, deformed bodies! Come out, you lepers and AIDS patients! Come out of your addictions—drug, alcohol, pornography, and murder! Lazarus, just come out! You will because Jesus said you would. This Lazarus Generation does have *hope*!

Perhaps you were taught, as I was, that you get one saved and then go on to the next one, then the next, and so on. But what did Jesus tell His disciples, Martha, and Mary? "Loose him!" (See John 11:44 KJV.) Why? Lazarus was still bound!

"But I was taught that when you're saved, you're saved. Right?" Yes, you are saved, but being ready for Heaven and being ready for a new life in this world are two different things. If not, then why was most of the New Testament written?

"Take Away the Stone"

I explained this matter of sanctification in my book, *Run Satan Run—But you Can't Hide!* See it for an in-depth study on sanctification.

More of the Bible is written on how to stay saved than on how to get saved. So let's learn how to unwrap a living, but bound up, generation.

First of all, it requires—actually demands—deliverance. They really need it. Do you realize how bad these folks smell? I'm not talking about physical body odor, but spiritual odor. Their thinking stinks.

At this point, let me give you a word of caution. Unless you've been delivered yourself, it would be better not to try delivering someone else. (Again, I suggest you read *Run Satan Run—But You Can't Hide!* on how to be set totally free.) In delivering people you will be faced with the following types of graveclothes:

1. Spirit of death and Hades: self-destruction or suicide.

2. Porno spirits, which have entered the minds of millions. Its manifestations include the following: lust, rape, incest, murder, etc., including suicide. How do they enter the minds? Through XXX-rated movies, video rentals, porno shops, home movies, cable TV. Porno shops are demon dens!

3. Kids whose minds have been robbed by arcades at our local malls. Parents, you need

to check these places out before you send your son or daughter into one. Don't let them go just because you're tired of messing with them.

4. The flesh.

5. Habits.

6. Strongholds.

7. Fear. This is a major area you'll face.

8. The past. This is also an important area.

9. Soul ties. Every time a person has *sex* with some new partner, his soul knits with them! (If it's a prostitute, mister, and not your wife, you are in big trouble. Try to guess how many other spirits you just took into your mind!)

In the unwrapping of Lazarus in Scripture, we see a good description of all the areas of life we deal with.

First, his face was covered. That represents the thought life. So we must help him get into the Word of God. For example, you could use Romans 12:1-2:

Therefore, I urge you, brothers, in view of God's mercy, to offer your bodies as living sacrifices, holy and pleasing to God—this is your spiritual act of worship. Do not conform any longer to the pattern of this world, but be transformed by the renewing of

"Take Away the Stone"

your mind. Then you will be able to test and approve what God's will is—His good, pleasing and perfect will (Romans 12:1-2).

Second, his hands were bound. That speaks of works, or a type of his character development. God told me some time ago, "You either have character, or you are one!" This is the very reason good men and women "go bad." They never allow the Holy Spirit to develop their characters! They think God said, "You can make it on charisma." What He really said was, "Let Me develop your character! Then you will have charisma." So many who have great charisma, but little character, are being slain by the enemy. We must stop the enemy from destroying these precious people! Let us learn how to set them free from the works of the flesh. Let's teach them how to be set free, absolutely free, in spirit, soul, and body as recorded in First Thessalonians 5:23-24.

Chapter 17

First Aid (Love) for Lazarus!

How-To's in Redeeming the Lazarus Generation

The dead man came out, his hands and feet wrapped with strips of linen, and a cloth around his face. Jesus said to them, "Take off the grave clothes and let him go" (John 11:44).

Jesus told *them*, which means *us* too, to "take off the grave clothes and let him go." That means "Let him go free"—free from all the things discussed in the previous chapter.

The Lazarus Generation

We must be the ones to let Lazarus go free. He said we are to do it! We've already established the fact that it's absolutely no fun at all. Still someone must do it, and it just so happens that Jesus chose the Church for the job. But aren't you glad you are the *deliverer* and not the victim being delivered? It could be the reverse. Nevertheless, this Lazarus Generation needs deliverance, a "first-aid" ministry. Deliverance teams are needed!

"You mean that *I* need to *deliver* people?"

Yes! Everyone—pastors, evangelists, teachers, prophets, apostles, and every other "real" Christian—needs to help. Don't leave this job solely to the five-fold people. Their function is to train the Church *how to* bring deliverance to people. (Read Ephesians 4:11-14.)

That's why, if you don't know how to bring deliverance, you should have your pastor show you. If he doesn't believe in it, go to him, in love, and ask him why he doesn't belive in it.

There's another parable in the Bible that tells us exactly how to render first aid to Lazarus:

> *On one occasion an expert in the law stood up to test Jesus. "Teacher," he asked, "what must I do to inherit eternal life?" "What is written in the Law?" He replied. "How do you read it?" He answered: " 'Love the Lord your God with all your heart and with all your soul and with all your strength and with all your mind'; and, 'Love your neighbor as yourself.' "*

First Aid (Love) for Lazarus!

"You have answered correctly," Jesus replied. "Do this and you will live." But he wanted to justify himself, so he asked Jesus, "And who is my neighbor?" In reply Jesus said: "A man was going down from Jerusalem to Jericho, when he fell into the hands of robbers. They stripped him of his clothes, beat him and went away, leaving him half dead. A priest happened to be going down the same road, and when he saw the man, he passed by on the other side. So too, a Levite, when he came to the place and saw him, passed by on the other side. But a Samaritan, as he traveled, came where the man was; and when he saw him, he took pity on him. He went to him and bandaged his wounds, pouring on oil and wine. Then he put the man on his own donkey, took him to an inn and took care of him. The next day he took out two silver coins and gave them to the innkeeper. 'Look after him,' he said, 'and when I return, I will reimburse you for any extra expense you may have.' Which of these three do you think was a neighbor to the man who fell into the hands of robbers?" The expert in the law replied, "The one who had mercy on him." Jesus told him, "Go and do likewise" (Luke 10:25-37).

Let me just comment a little. You can see that the self-righteous, religious bigots won't stop and help Lazarus. They didn't then, and they won't now. Only the "Good Samaritan" ministries of the world will help Lazarus. The "Good Samaritan" ministry is the first-aid or *deliverance* ministry.

This parable teaches us a vital principle. The Good Samaritan was a Gentile. We Gentiles will be the first to help. For instance, just look at the U.S.A. Who rallied first to help Kuwait, Vietnam, South Korea, Laos, Panama, or Bogota? You name it, and we have helped the poor and war-torn practically everywhere. And what about Israel? We Gentiles, Jesus lovers, faith-in-the-God-of-Abraham people, are the very same ones who scurried to stop a SCUD shot by Hussein. I shudder to think what would happen if there were no Good Samaritans in this world. Even Israel is an example (a recipient) of these Good Samaritans' work on earth!

As a first-aid or deliverance ministry, we must first place Lazarus in the inn: the Church, the Body of Christ. Take him to the inn; don't send him anywhere else! Place him in there and then see that he has everything he needs. *Deliverance* is first. *Development* or *discipleship* is second. *Delighting* or rejoicing is third—and yes, you will rejoice!

It is one thing to realize the spiritual deadness of this Lazarus Generation. It is another matter entirely to know how to help them. It's impossible to cover in detail everything the Church will face when setting Lazarus free from his graveclothes. However, the Holy Spirit has made it clear to me that there are two absolutes in redeeming Lazarus and seeing him totally set free—spirit, soul, and body.

The first absolute in seeing spiritual resurrection of this dying generation is God's love, His *agape*. It's

First Aid (Love) for Lazarus!

the pure, unadulterated, never-failing love of God. God's love in its purest form, flowing from His Church, is required in raising Lazarus from the dead. This same love is required to bring total deliverance and healing to such a person until he is finally restored to fullness of life.

The second absolute is a manifestation, or a demonstration, of the power of the *resurrection* of Jesus Christ. The full power of the resurrection that raised up Jesus from the dead is required and needs to be visibly demonstrated in these last days to raise both the Church and the world from their spiritual deadness. Both have been entombed by religion and are under judgment.

Without these two elements, the raising and unwrapping of Lazarus is impossible. Therefore we must learn about these two factors and how both are to be applied.

In order to firmly establish the process in our minds, let's review the order of ministry to Lazarus. First, we call him forth from the grave by the power of the resurrection and the pure love of God. This is his deliverance from the grave and the graveclothes. Second is his development, or discipleship. Please remember, though, that we can't develop him until we deliver him! First aid is first; then comes unwrapping him from his graveclothes.

As I stated previously, it is virtually impossible to deal with every issue and detail concerning the "how-to's" of delivering and discipling Lazarus in one chapter. Therefore I'll just lay a simple foundation to get you started. The Holy Spirit is your Teacher as well as mine, and He will instruct you on how to deal with this Lazarus Generation. After all, He is doing the same work worldwide!

Let me use an example that I feel the Spirit would have me share with you. It is about dealing with the *spirit of rejection* in this Lazarus Generation. "Bill" is a classic example of a young man who suffered beyond reason because of the *spirit of rejection*. He is part of a generation of people who felt that they had to earn their earthly fathers' love.

In many cases their fathers themselves suffered rejection from their fathers, and so on. These can be generational curses, where sins of the fathers are visited upon the third and fourth generations. This *spirit of rejection* can be stacked up three and four generations deep.

Bill was a victim of a generational spirit. His father was rejected, so the father passed it down to Bill. Bill tried to earn his father's love. He felt he had to do something worthwhile to have his father say those four simple but necessary words: "I love you, son." Instead he heard only these types of words: "How sorry you are," and "Get out of my face, you dummy."

The bottom line is this: We have an entire generation where the majority has never known the real love of an earthly father or ever heard a father say those simple, life-giving words: "I love you, son," or "I love you, daughter." This Lazarus Generation is starving for real love. They don't know *real love*, but they do know *real rejection*. Remember what God's Word says:

Because of the increase of wickedness, the love of most will grow cold (Matthew 24:12).

Here "love" is used in the original Greek as *agape*, God's love. So what was Jesus saying here in His prophetic word to the end-time generation that was to come? Verses 10-11 of that same chapter say:

At that time many will turn away from the faith and will betray and hate each other, and many false prophets will appear and deceive many people (Matthew 24:10-11).

Verse 12 shows the results of these two verses: wickedness will increase and so the love (*agape*) of *most* will *grow cold.*

Jesus was prophesying that in "that time," which is today, many people will, because of *offenses* in the Church, lose faith in God, or Christ. Remember, we live in a "*churchy world and a worldly church.*" People see the hypocrisy, double standards, and dual life styles and grow weary of it all. All the time they thought it was "true blue" Christianity.

Why does this happen? The genuine love of God, a fatherly love, cannot be found in the world or church that has shut out God (Jesus). If you had the world or a church operating strictly on a brotherly love (friendship love, *phileo* love), the type of love that says "I love my dog; I love my 4 x 4," it still would not work! Nothing short of God's love will save this lukewarm, Laodicean church world—a church world that brags of its wealth, buildings, programs, and need-of-nothing attitude.

Christ is at the door of His own church, knocking so He can enter and have true fellowship (intimacy) with us. Where did the relationship go wrong? Where did the problems start? Why has the Church, riddled with the world and its system, fallen into such a state? We have the answer right in the Word of God. Revelation 2:4 (AMP) says:

*But I have this [one charge to make] against you: that **you have left** (abandoned) the love that you had at first [**you have deserted Me, your first love**]* (Revelation 2:4 AMP).

Verse 5 says:

*Remember then from what heights **you have fallen. Repent**...do the works you did previously...or else I will visit you and **remove** your **lampstand** from its place...* (Revelation 2:5 AMP).

It all started in the first church period. The church in Ephesus fell from God's love to settle for a brotherly love (affection). It no longer practiced the Godly love of *self-sacrifice*. The church settled for works (labor) and not for God's best, which is *His rest*. That

First Aid (Love) for Lazarus!

is *rest* from our labors and trust (having faith) in His love, which is Jesus Himself! We need to become a Christ-centered church, not an ego-centered, I-centered church!

Recently the Holy Spirit told me that we must be a "theo-centric" church, not an "ego-centric" church. It is by *grace* that we are saved, not by *works*, lest we boast in ourselves (see Eph. 2:8-9).

Oh Laodicean church world, you are laden with good social works and programs; you are so refined and proper with wealth untold—yet you are neither cold nor hot, but *lukewarm* and satisfied with it all. You forget the reason for all of those works, programs, and labors: Jesus! He alone can satisfy the lonely and sin-sick soul. Only His love can raise this spiritually dying and dead generation. However, there's one major problem. He's not in most of our churches anymore. You may have what you call "church," but He has visited you and removed your candlestick. His Holy Spirit is no longer in your church. Notice I said "your church," not "His church." Jesus does have a Church, and you will recognize it by two things: it will have His unfailing, fatherly love and His resurrection power as the center of its focus.

Bill, our example, was a victim in a vacuum void of God's love because the church world was not manifesting *His love* to a dying world. Bill tried hard to earn his father's love, but never seemed to merit it. Bill achieved much in high school sports, and football in particular. He even received a scholarship to play for a college team. Then he made it to a semi-pro team on the West Coast where there was glamor, fame, money, women, sex, booze, and parties. Yet all of that didn't bring these simple words into reality: "I love you, son. You're doing great. I'm proud of you."

Bill then got into body building. He was not just your mediocre macho hunk; Bill could bench press 500 pounds, and he took several first place trophies, tall and shiny. Still there was no "I love you, son." Many multitudes like Bill have yet to hear those words from an earthly father. Unfortunately, for many it's too late. They were abused and used by their fathers but never loved.

As I was writing this chapter and preparing this material for a Sunday message, the Holy Spirit spoke these sad words to me: "These are not children who were *aborted* by their mothers *before* their birth, but they were *abandoned* by their fathers *after* their birth." Orphans in their own houses, they were left to *wonder* what true love is all about and to *wander* about seeking it on their own. Even worse, they became deceived into believing that *they* had done something wrong, and therefore it was *their* fault that *they* were rejected.

Rejection from an earthly father has caused more hurt and sorrow in the lives of this Lazarus Generation than any other thing I know of. Some may say, "I was never rejected by my earthly father; it was my mother who rejected me." What you may fail to recognize is the root of that rejection. Probably your mother suffered rejection too, and most likely it was from her father. Thus it's still a problem with a father who rejected his child.

In 30 years of counselling people as a pastor, the problem of rejection stands out as one of the greatest. So many people's problems stem from rejection from a parent who was rejected by his/her own father and, in turn, passed the rejection on to his/her children. This lack of a father's love has caused the spirit of rejection to dominate the lives of millions of children. This spirit will virtually dominate their whole beings and behavior for their entire lives if it's not dealt with by God's love and power.

Thus the absence of the love of a father is the root from which the fruit of rejection grew. When a father abuses a child (that abuse can be in many forms), he is sending a strong message to his child that says, "I don't really love you. I may be fond of you, but I don't love you." This is too true, or he would never have an incestuous relationship with that daughter. Nor would he verbally batter that boy with cruel words like these: "You dumb idiot, you're not worth spit! Get out of my face!" Many times such words are accompanied by a physical blow to the head.

Here is the second part in the sad saga of the rejected child. Most of the time this rejection and lack of love from an earthly father gives the children the impression that they are also rejected and unloved by their heavenly Father, the One who created them.

"Did I hear you correctly? They feel rejected by God, their heavenly Father?"

Yes. You see, this earthly father we refer to is usually a "religious" man. He is a "church goer" and may have a strong "religious" background. He could even be a deacon or a Sunday School teacher. He may even pay his tithe and never miss a Sunday morning service or revival meeting.

Religion knows *about* God, but a relationship with God *knows* God and knows He is love! Therefore, if an earthly father knows only *about* God, then he has religion. Religion is not righteousness (right standing with God) or peace and joy in the Holy Ghost. That father is only relating "religion," not "righteousness," to his children. Nevertheless, they receive and perceive it as what their heavenly Father is also like.

Rejection tops the list as one of the greatest deceptions and tools the devil ever used to destroy God the Father's true character. That character is *agape* love; true love toward us forever!

It would require volumes to relate what damage religion, not righteousness, has caused in the home. Religion's effort to relate God's love is futile when fathers have not experienced true love from God the Father for themselves. Those who are into religion and not relationship fail miserably in acting like the heavenly Father; they wind up acting like their real father, the devil. So remember this: God the Father's real love will never be seen in our children until we ourselves have a true relationship with our heavenly Father.

To reach this Lazarus Generation, we need the pure form of the love of God the Father. That love must, of necessity, come from Him to us, the Church. It is *in* us first, then it flows *through* us, the Church, to this dying, hurting, rejected generation. This Lazarus Generation, as victims of rejection, think they must do something or be something special, something spectacular, or be spotless, to be accepted by man and God. They perceive God to be angry, abusive, cruel, and dictatorial, like their earthly (devilish) father. I have heard so many say, "If God's anything like my ol' man, I don't want to get acquainted with Him. I don't need more rejection: I need someone to love me and accept me as I am."

Despite all this deception and beguilement the devil has used with people in religion to distort our heavenly Father's true character, Jesus stands at the door today, ready to return to His Church if we will only open and let Him in! He alone is able and ready to reveal the Father's true character of love to this Lazarus Generation. His Father is loving and kind; He is forgiving and waiting anxiously for the return of this prodigal world and the church world. Without hidden agenda (there's no burden of do's and don't's), He awaits His wayward sons and daughters with wide open and outstretched arms and sparkling eyes filled with a father's love—a love beyond words or worlds unknown!

Yet the question still remains: How will this generation see that fatherly love? How will they have a true image of the Father?

The answer is this: They will see His love through you and me. So let's be about the Father's business of demonstrating His love and resurrection power to this Lazarus Generation. They've been rejected by their earthly fathers' love, but never by their heavenly Father's true love! "For God so loved the world, that He gave His only begotten Son, that whosoever believeth in Him should not perish [for lack of love], but have everlasting life [through God's love, demonstrated by the power of the resurrection]" (Jn. 3:16 KJV).

Let us radiate His love, the love of God, the Father of lights, in whom is no darkness or shadow of turning! (See James 1:17.) It is impossible for God to change (see Mal. 3:6), and God is love (see 1 John 4:8,16). His resurrection power also is forever. So, Lazarus—come forth! God loves you, and so do we! For His love abides in us, and we have His power to prove it!

As a reminder, Church: "Remember then from what heights you have fallen. Repent...and do the works you did previously..." (Rev. 2:5 AMP). That work was to see Jesus and be like Him, who is love manifested in the flesh.

The answer to the salvation of you and your Lazarus children, or a possible pending judgment (for the curse continues), is found in God's Word. This judgment will only wax worse if we fail to repent of our dead works and refuse to return to God's unfailing love as our standard for life and as our tool for ministering to this Lazarus Generation. Here is God's final word on this matter:

> *See, I will send you the prophet Elijah before that great and dreadful day of the Lord comes. He will turn the hearts of the **fathers** to their **children**, and the hearts of the **children** to their **fathers**; or else I will come and strike the land with a curse* (Malachi 4:5-6).

The following pages contain an outline "How-To" for developing growth in Lazarus. It is very simple, but very effective.

NOTE: Also see *Run, Satan, Run—But You Can't Hide!* (by Samuel L. Brassfield, published by Companion Press, copyright 1992) for a more in-depth study. It is this Lazarus Generation, spoken of in the Word of God, that becomes that mighty, militant, fighting machine for God that reaches this world for Jesus.

So here is an example of a simple development *outline* that I gave to a Lazarus Generation convert:

The Lazarus Generation

To Bill

From Your Friend and Pastor, Samuel Brassfield

Please use the Living Bible:

2 Corinthians 5:17

1. When someone becomes a Christian, he becomes a brand-new person *inside*. He is *not* the same anymore.

2. Question:How did I become a Christian?

    Answer:Romans 10:8-10

3. Question:Now that I am a Christian...what?

    Answer:Romans 8:1-16
    Romans 8:24-39

4. Question:How do I *behave* as a Christian?

    Answer:Romans 12:1-5

5. So you need help to know these things and then to do them to please God, who saved you.

    Question:How do I study and understand God's Word, the Bible? Who will help me pray, study, and understand God's Word?

    Answer:The Holy Spirit. He is your new friend to help you, guide you, and teach you about the Father and Jesus, your Savior and Lord. Romans 8:26

First Aid (Love) for Lazarus!

6. The Trinity: The Father, The Son (Jesus), and the Holy Spirit.

7. Spirit: The Holy Spirit is now living in you, since you became a Christian by accepting Christ into your heart by faith. Romans 10:8-10

Romans 8:9-17 tells us how the Holy Spirit will help us, now and forever! It tells how the Holy Spirit dwells in your heart, or spirit.

Bill, you are a spirit (God-like).

You have a soul (will, intellect [mind], emotions).

You live in a body (physical, temple, flesh)
1 Thessalonians 5:16-24; (key verse: 23)
(I will talk more about this to you later.)

*Love

The Holy Spirit (Romans 8:12-16) will help us and teach us how to live so we won't perish. The *old way* was leading us to certain death, sin, sickness, disease, hell, torment, fear, lust, pride.... It brought us to all kinds of bondage, none of which produced joy, peace, fulfillment, or life. But now, because of Jesus, who is *God's true "love"* in a personage, (Jn. 3:16), we are now made *free* from sin.

Now that we are free, we must learn how to stay free from sin, which was bringing us certain death. Galatians 5:1 says that Christ has made us free. Now we must *make sure* that we *stay free*.

Galatians 5:5 says, "But we by the help of the Holy Spirit are counting on Christ's death to clear away our sins and make us right with God."

✸ Galatians 5:6 says, "...for all we need is *faith* working through *love*." It is *God's love* for us, through our faith or trust in Christ.

Romans 10:17 says, "Yet faith comes from listening to this Good News—the Good News about Christ." In other words, faith comes from listening to God's Word, the Bible, which tells us about Jesus—who He is and what He has done for us. So we must read, study, and learn about Jesus through God's Word by the help of the Holy Spirit, our new Teacher.

In John 16:5-15 Jesus tells us about the Holy Spirit; that the Holy Spirit is our Guide, Teacher, Instructor, etc. He will show us the way to God and what God's will and plan are for us. He will make us happy, healthy, and fulfilled, not only in this life, but forever with Him in the world to come!

✸ Galatians 5:13 speaks about our new freedom. We have this new freedom not to do wrong again, but to *love* and serve each other!

✸ Galatians 5:14 tells us about God's law: "*Love* others as you *love* yourself."

First Aid (Love) for Lazarus!

Galatians 5:16 says, "I advise you to obey only the Holy Spirit's instructions...." Remember, He is our new Instructor. He will *never* leave us alone.

8. Read the following Scripture passage for help in seeing what is happening in your spirit, soul, and body at this point:

   Galatians 5:16-23. The Holy Spirit will tell you where to go and what to do. Then you won't always be doing the wrong things your *old nature* was doing that brought you pain, sorrow, sadness, fear, death, etc.

9. Question: What happens when we follow our own wrong inclinations (desires)?

   Answer: It will produce these *evil* results, and thus *death*.

10. Question: What happens when we follow the Holy Spirit and let Him control our lives for Jesus?

    Answer: Look at the difference to see how much better the results are when you allow *God's love*, through Jesus, into your life. See how much better it is to allow the Holy Spirit to help you in this life. The final results are what you desired *all along*, and looked for and tried to find: *love*, joy, peace, etc. Read Galatians 5:22-23 and see!

The Lazarus Generation

I will close for now, but will continue to help you and guide you as your *friend* and *pastor*. Just call any time. I'll be here for you, my friend.

> In Christ's Love,
> Pastor B.

My private office phone:
My home phone:

Another person who will help you if I am not around is _____ .

His work phone:
His home phone:

Call any time, day or night.

Chapter 18

Believer or "Rat-Fink" Religionist?

Therefore many of the Jews who had come to visit Mary, and had seen what Jesus did, put their faith in Him. But some of them went to the Pharisees and told them what Jesus had done. Then the chief priests and the Pharisees called a meeting of the Sanhedrin. "What are we accomplishing?" they asked. "Here is this man performing many miraculous signs. If we let Him go on like this, everyone will believe in Him, and then the Romans will come and take away both our place and our nation" (John 11:45-48).

Some Jews put their faith (trust) in Jesus; some Jews went to the Pharisees and *told* them what Jesus had done. Then the chief priests and Pharisees called a meeting of the infamous Sanhedrin. Doesn't it sound familiar? It sounds just like a worldwide council of churches or some denominations' meetings.

The question these Jews asked themselves was this: "What are we accomplishing?" Then they answered their own question: absolutely nothing! "If we let Him go on like this, *everyone* will believe in Him." Folks, that's the objective! That was His purpose, and it should be ours as well!

This is a vital key to world evangelism. Even the "very religious" know the answer—that if Jesus is allowed to continue like this (raising the dead, performing signs and wonders), then *everyone will believe in Him. Praise The Lord!*

A ministry of signs and wonders is a *must*. Religionists today say, "Oh, the days of signs and wonders are over, don't you know?"

Wake up and live! That was Jesus' "calling card" to His generation, and so it must be in ours to the Lazarus Generation! (See Acts 2:22.)

I'm going to be bold and say this: "If you don't believe in signs and wonders and expect them in your church services today, then you will before long!" You will believe one way or the other. You will either have a ministry of signs and wonders like Jesus did, or you will have a "For Sale" sign in front of your church or denominational headquarters. Don't laugh at this prophecy today, or you may see a sign "about this time" tomorrow—your "For Sale" *sign*—and *wonder* what has happened. These are not joking matters. If you despise prophecy or quench the Holy Spirit in your church services, you will wind up as sold to satan's trap of compromise and complacency.

"And then the Romans will come and take away both our place and our nation." Only it won't be the Romans this time; it will be the *righteous*. They will literally take the place and the kingdom of the unrighteous. They will take their neighborhoods, their schools, their businesses, their wealth, and their world! God's Word said it! Just read Daniel's vision and prophecy of Nebuchadnezzar's image, the image of feet of iron and clay.

While you were watching, a rock was cut out, but not by human hands. It struck the statue on its feet of iron and clay and smashed them. Then the iron, the clay, the bronze, the silver and the gold were broken to pieces at the same time and became like chaff on a threshing floor in the summer. The wind swept them away without leaving a trace. But the rock that struck the statue became a huge mountain and filled the whole earth (Daniel 2:34-35).

In the time of those kings, the God of heaven will set up a kingdom that will never be destroyed, nor will it be left to another people. It will crush all those kingdoms and bring them to an end, but it will itself endure forever. This is the meaning of the vision of the rock cut out of a mountain, but not by human hands—a rock that broke the iron, the bronze, the clay, the silver and the gold to pieces… (Daniel 2:44-45).

What was prophesied would happen to it? Jesus, "the Rock," rolled over it like a huge tractor trailer! Peter, in his first epistle, writes about "the Rock" that Daniel saw:

As you come to Him, the living Stone—rejected by men but chosen by God and precious to Him—you also, like living stones, are being built into a spiritual house to be a holy priesthood, offering spiritual sacrifices acceptable to God through Jesus Christ. For in Scripture it says: "See, I lay a stone in Zion, a chosen and precious cornerstone, and the one who trusts in Him will never be put to shame." Now to you who believe, this stone is precious. But to those who do not believe, "The stone the builders rejected has become the capstone," and, "A stone that causes men to stumble and a rock that makes them fall." They stumble because they disobey the message—which is also what they were destined for (1 Peter 2:4-8).

That's what happened; so shall it be today! The Romans won't take over the "religious," but the righteous will.

Chapter 19

Prophecy Fulfilled— The Restoration of the Rascals

Then one of them, named Caiaphas, who was high priest that year, spoke up, "You know nothing at all! You do not realize that it is better for you that one man die for the people than that the whole nation perish." He did not say this on his own, but as high priest that year he prophesied that Jesus would die for the Jewish nation, and not only for that nation but also for the scattered children of God, to bring them together and make them one. So from that day on they plotted to take His life (John 11:49-53).

Prophecy has been fulfilled; the children will not die. The prodigals, the outcasts of Israel, will come home. These *are* the first fruits of this last-days revival and restoration of *all things*. These prodigals are a great part of this world harvest! (Remember this is not just for natural Israel, dear reader.)

Caiaphas prophesied of the restoration of the scattered children of God. Yes, one of those "religious rascals" said it! They spoke of this final day out of their own mouths, yet they didn't even come close to seeing what they were helping God fulfill. Caiaphas spoke to those who were about to crucify Jesus our Lord, the Sanhedrin court of his day, and unknowingly spoke centuries into the future to our final generation, this Lazarus Generation.

Caiaphas first said, "You know nothing at all!" How true his statement was! They knew nothing about what was to happen. They did not know that it was not only for them then, but also for us now! He also said, "You do not realize that it is better for you that *one man die* for the people [them and us] than that the *whole nation perish*." Here he not only prophesied for their salvation, but also for that of our *nations*—America, Australia, Russia, all the European nations, African nations, the Eastern nations, etc.—for the whole world!

Prophecy Fulfilled—The Restoration of the Rascals

The Bible says, "He did not say this on his own, but as high priest that year he *prophesied* that Jesus would die for the *Jewish nation*, and not only for that nation but also for the *scattered* children of God, to bring them *together* and *make them one*" (Jn. 11:51-52).

This prophecy has not yet been fulfilled in the earth, but we will see it fulfilled in our day, this last-day hour. He is gathering the "outcasts of Israel" and Father Abraham's spiritual seed, which all together number as the sand of the sea and the stars of the heavens! By the way, God hasn't lost sight of that prophecy either. That was *His* promise to Abraham and Caiaphas, the high priest. We know that God never breaks His promises!

Don't think it won't happen just because it hasn't yet. That's what Abraham thought, but when he was 100 years old, it happened just like Father God said. Isaac was born to a dead womb and a past-age father. People said Lazarus was dead too! But when Jesus, The I Am, spoke to the dead who had believed in Him who would die and rise again, also "Come forth from the dead and live again," it happened! So shall it be with this last-days' Lazarus Generation, which is considered dead. Out of a generation of doom and gloom, out of a spiritually dead womb, a spiritually impotent leadership (clergy, preachers, pastors, priests), and dead denominations, will come forth the greatest spiritual birth in the history of the world! We need to get ready for it! As the prophet Joel said, "...Your sons and daughters will prophesy, your old men will dream dreams, your young men will see visions. Even on my servants, both men and women, I will pour out My spirit in those days" (Joel 2:28-29; see also Acts 2:17-18).

We will see the restoration of the prodigals, as prophesied.

The same "spirit of prophecy" that was upon Caiaphas is speaking again today. As the high priest prophesied in *that year* that Jesus would die, the same spirit of prophecy is in this year saying that Jesus did die (past tense) for that nation and that He did die (past tense) for the scattered *children of God*, to bring (future tense) *them* now (present tense) *together* and make them *one*.

We have not become one yet; at least, I have not read about it in church history or seen it in my day. So that means only one thing: it must happen before long, if Jesus' coming is soon!

The skeptics and doubters of this last-day revival and restoration message say, "Will Jesus come? Will He show up at the Passover? Is He coming as He promised He would?" John 11:56 tells us that the people kept looking for Jesus and asking the question of one another, "What do you think? Isn't He coming to the Feast at all?" Will Jesus show up at the memorial supper of the Lamb? Will He, as the Bridegroom, show up as He stated? Oh, how many times we have heard, "Behold, the bridegroom cometh; go ye out to meet him" (Mt. 25:6 KJV).

"Is it true, Preacher? Will He come again? Soon? Oh, I hurt so bad, Preacher. I have so many loved ones who are lost, sir. There are so many still to become saved. Is there *still hope* for salvation? For the gathering of all the outcasts of Israel, the seed of Abraham, who will be called the children of God? Of all my scattered children who are still in sin and sorrow, is there any *hope* that they will be gathered before Jesus comes?"

The answer is *yes*, my friends. Your prodigals will return home to the Father's house. It's the greatest news you will ever hear, so get ready! Whatever has happened in the natural, that which we've read about in the Word of God, will also be fulfilled in the spiritual.

Chapter 20

Will Jesus Come to the Dinner?

Six days before the Passover, Jesus arrived at Bethany, where Lazarus lived, whom Jesus had raised from the dead. **Here a dinner was given in Jesus' honor.** *Martha served, while Lazarus was among those reclining at the table with Him. Then Mary took about a pint of pure nard, an expensive perfume; she poured it on Jesus' feet and wiped His feet with her hair. And the house was filled with the fragrance of the perfume* (John 12:1-3).

"*Six days* before the Passover, Jesus *arrived* at Bethany, where Lazarus lived, whom Jesus had raised from the dead." Did you see that? Six days—six thousand years—before the Passover, Jesus arrived at Bethany! He will come back at the appointed time, just in time for the Passover feast!

Jesus raised (past tense) Lazarus from the dead. In this spiritual analogy, that means this Lazarus Generation shall be saved, raised from this planet of doom and despair, sin and sickness, and disease and poverty. You see, Lazarus was not dead in the tomb, but sleeping—just like Jesus said!

At this dinner given in Jesus' honor, Martha *served*. Martha is a type of those in the Church who believe in the resurrection; moreover, who believe Jesus is the resurrection and that He would raise Lazarus from the dead, spiritually.

Lazarus was there too, *among* those reclining at the table with Jesus. This Lazarus Generation, the "former dead," shall be raised up to eat with Jesus at His table and lean on His breast. The skeptics, the doubters, said it couldn't be done!

"Then Mary took about a pint of pure nard, an expensive perfume; she poured it on Jesus' feet and wiped His feet with her hair. And the house was filled with the fragrance of the perfume." What an analogy! When we praise and worship in *spirit* and in *truth* at Jesus' feet, the whole house is filled with praise and worship. Our true worship and praise then becomes a sweet odor to Jesus.

Will Jesus Come to the Dinner?

The only way you and I can make it is through a personal relationship at Jesus' feet. Mary and Martha both were there at the supper, but guess who also was there—the Lazarus Generation!

John 12:9 states that "a large crowd of Jews found out that Jesus was there and came, not only because of Him *but also to see Lazarus, whom He had raised from the dead."*

The punch line is in verse 11: "...many of the Jews *were going over* to Jesus and putting their faith in Him." Did you see it? Today's Jews are about to "go over" to Jesus, to the so-called Gentile Jesus. Moreover, they will put their faith in Him! They too will see their Messiah's return. Return? They may think He is about to come for the first time, but He actually is about to come for the second time.

John 12:12-13 says that Jesus was found on *His way* to Jerusalem. They, the Jews, took palm branches and went out to meet Him, shouting! "Hosanna! Blessed is He who comes in the name of the Lord! Blessed is the King of Israel!"

Nation of Israel, do not be afraid of your natural enemies. See, your King is coming! He is not seated on a donkey's colt this time, but on a white horse, as seen in the Book of Revelation. Jesus Christ is the "Lord of lords" and "King of kings" (see Rev. 17:14; 19:16). John 12:16 tells us that His disciples at first didn't understand what was happening. Only after Jesus was glorified did they realize that these things had been (past tense) about Him—and that these things (the crucifixion) had been done to Him. But we all, including the Jews, will before long see Him glorified among the nations of the whole earth!

Seed of Abraham, "Hear ye the word of the Lord," as spoken by one of your own prophets:

Arise, shine, for your light has come, and the glory of the Lord rises upon you. See, darkness covers the earth and thick darkness is over the peoples, but the Lord rises upon you and His glory appears over you. Nations will come to your light, and kings to the brightness of your dawn (Isaiah 60:1-3).

Foreigners will rebuild your walls, and their kings will serve you. Though in anger I struck you, in favor I will show you compassion. Your gates will always stand open, they will never be shut, day or night, so that men may bring you the wealth of the nations—their kings led in triumphal procession. For the nation or kingdom that will not serve you will perish; it will be utterly ruined. The glory of Lebanon will come to you, the pine, the fir and the cypress together, to adorn the place of my sanctuary; and I will glorify the place of my feet. The sons of your oppressors will come bowing before you; all who despise you will bow down at your feet and will call you the city of the Lord, Zion of the Holy One of Israel (Isaiah 60:10-14).

Will Jesus Come to the Dinner?

Then I looked up—and there before me was a man with a measuring line in his hand! I asked, "Where are you going?" He answered me, "To measure Jerusalem, to find out how wide and how long it is." Then the angel who was speaking to me left, and another angel came to meet him and said to him: "Run, tell that young man, 'Jerusalem will be a city without walls because of the great number of men and livestock in it. And I Myself will be a wall of fire around it,' declares the Lord, 'and I will be its glory within'" (Zechariah 2:1-5).

These passages speak of the restoration of Israel and the coming glory of the God of Abraham, Isaac, and Jacob (Israel), but please see the other side of this coin of God's great grace. Allow what Paul spoke in the New Testament Book of Romans to be applied *first* to the Gentiles, for it surely will be! With all respect to the twenty-first century nation of Israel and the Israel since the time of Moses, the prophet of God, the vast and great nations of the Gentiles will be gathered first by your and our Father, Jehovah God. Soon the glory of the Lord will be upon the Gentiles and oh, how great is that glory! Many nations from all over the world will come to God's glorious light—the light of Christ, the true Messiah of both Jew and Gentile. God said it through one of Israel's own prophets!

But, nation of Israel, you are not left without *hope*. Sing! There is a *great hope* for you whose people live in fear of missiles, who live in fear of more attacks from surrounding nations. Don't fear them, O people of Israel; God's love and mercy are forever. Read His Word; He gave it to you first. Please don't make the same mistake as your forefathers of rejecting Him.

> *Now the crowd that was with Him when He called Lazarus from the tomb and raised him from the dead continued to spread the word. Many people, because they had heard that He had given this miraculous sign, went out to meet Him. So the Pharisees said to one another, "See, this is getting us nowhere. Look how the whole world has gone after Him!"* (John 12:17-19)

The *whole world* will experience this gathering of Gentiles and Jews to the Messiah!

Our sons and daughters shall prophesy! Our prodigals will come home! This is the beginning of this last-day revival and harvest of the restoration of *all things.* Now is the time to rejoice and shout, for salvation is come worldwide! (See Acts 3:17-21.)

In the parable of the prodigal son, in Luke 15:11-32, the three players are the father, the older son, and the younger son. Verse 23 speaks of "the fattened calf." The key verse in the account in James 5:1-11, verse 5, says, "...You have fattened yourselves in the day of slaughter." Then note this: "But the wealth of the sinner is stored up for the righteous" (Prov. 13:22b NKJ). Period. The wealth is the fatted calf! Great wealth is coming to the Church! Why? To finance this great Gentile harvest!

Church, we must make a choice! Will we rejoice with the servants, the father, and the prodigal Lazarus Generation? Or will we "be mad, not glad," like the older son in his self-pity (pious) party? Is not the real party in the camp of the righteous?

We must have new wine in new wineskins (see Mt. 9:17), or we will swell up and pop while the true Church rejoices with the angels in Heaven over the prodigal Lazarus Generation. "My son, your brother was dead, but *now* he is alive."

This new wave of God is being carefully watched by traditional religion. (It's the story of old school versus the new move!) So we must choose wisely.

Chapter 21

A Final Word on the Final Restoration

One Sabbath, when Jesus went to eat in the house of a prominent Pharisee, **He was being carefully watched**. *There in front of Him was a man suffering from dropsy. Jesus asked the Pharisees and experts in the law, "Is it lawful to heal on the Sabbath or not?" But they remained silent. So taking hold of the man, He healed him and sent him away. Then He asked them, "If one of you has a son or an ox that falls into a well on the Sabbath day, will you not immediately pull him out?" And they had nothing to say* (Luke 14:1-6).

Are we religious or righteous? We must choose now. Jesus was carefully watched. Why? Religion (the law keepers) always prefers the "letter of the law" over mercy, love, kindness, goodness, grace, etc. Human need is *never* more important to the religious than their rules and regulations.

Jesus was being carefully watched, and in front of Him was a man suffering from dropsy. Jesus our Lord is love, mercy, grace, kindness, salvation, healing, deliverance, life, peace, giving, and much more! How did He handle these "religious experts" in the law? He posed two questions:

"Is it lawful to heal on the Sabbath or not?" and "If one of you has a son or an ox that falls into a well on the Sabbath day, will you not immediately pull him out?" For both questions they remained silent, and had nothing to say.

They didn't answer the first question because they wanted to trap Jesus into breaking the Law of Moses. Then they would have had a legal right to expose Him as a fraud. But Jesus, being Almighty God in the flesh and knowing what is in the heart of man (see Mt. 9:4), quickly asked the second question. With the man healed and sent away, Jesus' second question got Him past the so-called religious experts and actually snared them in their own trap.

How did He do that? In His question He mentioned a son and an ox. A son represented the pride of the father. An ox represented man's livelihood—food, clothing, and shelter. If his oxen died, so would he and his family. If his son died, all his hopes and dreams for the next generation would fade. So of course it was lawful to heal on the Sabbath. Jesus had out-foxed the most religious spirits of His day—and we will too!

In Luke 14:7-14, Jesus prepares us for the "upcoming" banquet. He tells us that upon receiving the invitation, we are to not pick a place of honor. Picking the honorable place speaks of self-pride, self-worth, and self-righteousness. The Word warns us: "...Do not think of yourself more highly than you ought..." (Rom. 12:3), and "Pride goes before destruction, a haughty spirit before a fall" (Prov. 16:18).

In Luke 14:11, Jesus lets us know that "everyone who exalts himself will be humbled, and he who humbles himself will be exalted." There is a vast difference between humbling oneself and being humbled!

Verses 12-14 instruct us whom we are to invite to a luncheon or dinner: "...do not invite your friends, your brothers or relatives, or your rich neighbors; if you do, they may invite you back and so you will be repaid. But when you give a banquet, invite the poor, the crippled, the lame, the blind, and you will be blessed. Although they cannot repay you, you will be repaid at the resurrection of the righteous." We must feed those who are poor, sickly, and hurting—those who can't even think of rewarding us or returning an invitation. These are the street people, the transients, the bag people of our city. We must provide them with clothing, food, and shelter. We must visit the sick in our city and heal them! We are to heal the poor who are sick, every one of them! Feed the hungry. Clothe the naked. Support the widows and orphans. These are all part of the Lazarus Generation. These are commandments of the Lord, not options!

Luke 14:15-24 talk about the great banquet itself. It is being prepared now. The invitation has been sent out, saying, "Come, for everything is now ready" (v. 17). Who will make excuses? The dividing has begun; the wheat is being separated from the tares and all those who will go into the great banquet from all who will not go in! The true harvest is now being separated from the tares, who are the religious, not the righteous!

Everyone, from this day forward, who makes excuses for not coming to the banquet has *religious spirits*. We are not to worry about them. When you invite someone to come to Jesus and he responds with a "yes," then good. Lead that person into God's house. If he responds with a "no," then leave that person alone! Don't waste your time casting your pearls before swine! (See Matthew 7:6.) If an individual makes excuses, let him; you keep on going to another, and another, and another. Don't stop or waste time! None of those who refuse will taste the banquet. None of them will get the double anointing, the final perfecting, and the blessings that are included in the banquet.

We must go to the Lazarus Generation, into the streets and alleys of the city, and bring in the poor, the crippled, the blind, and the lame, (both physically and spiritually, for they are all the same in God's eyes). Luke 14:21-22 tell us that when we have done that, there will still be room for more. However, first we must make sure that we obeyed the Lord's foremost command: We don't stop until the house of the Lord is full (Lk. 14:23). The house of the Lord must be filled! This is a mandate, not an option!

Chapter 22

A Last Word on the Restoration of Lazarus

"Total" or "complete" restoration of *all things* is coming! Get ready, Church!

The Holy Spirit chooses to use an Old Testament event to illustrate a last word on the final restoration to the Church and this final generation, the Lazarus Generation.

David asked, "Is there anyone still left of the house of Saul to whom I can show kindness for Jonathan's sake?" Now there was a servant of Saul's household named Ziba. They called him to appear before David, and the king said to him, "Are you Ziba?" "Your servant," he replied. The king asked, "Is there no one still left of the house of Saul to whom I can show God's kindness?" Ziba answered the king, "There is still a son of Jonathan; he is crippled in both feet." "Where is he?" the king asked. Ziba answered, "He is at the house of Makir son of Ammiel in Lo Debar." So King David had him brought from Lo Debar, from the house of Makir son of Ammiel. When Mephibosheth son of Jonathan, the son of Saul, came to David, he bowed down to pay him honor. David said, "Mephibosheth!" "Your servant," he replied. "Don't be afraid," David said to him, "for I will surely show you kindness for the sake of your father Jonathan. I will restore to you all the land that belonged to your grandfather Saul, and you will always eat at my table." Mephibosheth bowed down and said, "What is your servant, that you should notice a dead dog like me?" Then the king summoned Ziba, Saul's servant, and said to him, "I have given your master's grandson everything that belonged to Saul and his family. You and your sons and your servants are to farm the land for him and bring in the crops, so that your master's grandson may be provided for. And Mephibosheth, grandson of your master, will always eat at my table." (Now Ziba had fifteen sons and twenty servants.) Then Ziba said to the king, "Your servant will do whatever my lord the

A Last Word on the Restoration of Lazarus

king commands his servant to do." So Mephibosheth ate at David's table like one of the king's sons. Mephibosheth had a young son named Mica, and all the members of Ziba's household were servants of Mephibosheth. And Mephibosheth lived in Jerusalem, because he always ate at the king's table, and he was crippled in both feet (2 Samuel 9).

This is the story of a "final restoration" of all the promises made in a blood covenant between David and Jonathan, Saul's son (see 1 Sam. 18:1-4; 19:1,4; 20:1-16). Especially in First Samuel 18:1-4 and 20:14-17 we can see this covenant between David and Jonathan:

After David had finished talking with Saul, Jonathan became one in spirit with David, and he loved him as himself. From that day Saul kept David with him and did not let him return to his father's house. And Jonathan made a covenant with David because he loved him as himself. Jonathan took off the robe he was wearing and gave it to David, along with his tunic, and even his sword, his bow and his belt (1 Samuel 18:1-4).

"But show me unfailing kindness like that of the Lord as long as I live, so that I may not be killed, and do not ever cut off your kindness from my family— not even when the Lord has cut off every one of David's enemies from the face of the earth." So Jonathan made a covenant with the house of David, saying, "May the Lord call David's enemies to account." And Jonathan had David reaffirm his oath out of love for him,

because he loved him as he loved himself (1 Samuel 20:14-17).

Let us look first at the fulfillment of this covenant and then at the blood covenant God made with us, which He cut with our "father of faith," Abraham. We will soon see this blood covenant fulfilled, for God always keeps His promises.

Second Samuel 9:1-13, the story of Mephibosheth, reveals the fulfillment of the covenant between David and Jonathan. It was written to show us what God is about to do in this Lazarus Generation. Total restoration is coming!

Saul had been appointed King of Israel, but he failed to obey God's Word. Thus he was rejected as king. (See First Samuel 15.) Samuel, the prophet of God, was called by the Lord to go and anoint David as the next King of Israel. The anointing had departed from Saul and he ruled Israel by the flesh, not the spirit. (See First Samuel 16.) As you can read in the Scriptures, it was death for Saul and pure hell for Israel until David was released by the Spirit to lead Israel—even before he was actually appointed king. David was highly favored by God and by Saul's own son, Jonathan, who was next in line, naturally speaking, to inherit the throne from Saul. But God had another plan, for He had found a man after His own heart: David! (See First Samuel 13:14 and Acts 13:22.)

A Last Word on the Restoration of Lazarus

From David's descendants came Jesus' earthly father! Hallelujah! We too are of the same covenant!

Saul and Jonathan were both killed in a fleshly battle. They were destroyed in the flesh, by the flesh. (The flesh will kill you; it is no respecter of persons!) After great struggles, David was finally king. But he also remembered where he came from and how he came to be king. He knew well that he had been protected by the covenant he had made with his friend Jonathan. So he would *now* fulfill all of his promises, no matter how bad the past, no matter how cruel Saul had been. Past memories were now faded into oblivion. Remember, David is a man after God's *own* heart. Remember too that he is a type of Jesus Christ, our Lord, who is a prophet, priest, and king!

David represents Jesus and poor crippled Mephibosheth represents us—this Lazarus Generation. That means we do have *hope*, that we are not forgotten by God. He will keep His blood covenant promises. He has not failed us. He does remember what He has promised. And that is absolute, true, and perfectly wonderful restoration!

David asked, (Jesus asks the Father), "Is there anyone still left of the house of Saul (house of flesh), to whom I can show mercy, kindness, and unconditional love, for Jonathan's sake (the blood covenant's sake)?"

Ziba answered the king (Jesus): "There is still a son of Jonathan; he is crippled in both feet."

"Where is he?" the king (Jesus) asked.

This Lazarus Generation is sick, and they're out there in the gay bars, hell holes, alleys, prostitutes' corners, massage parlors, etc. They're crippled and living outside of God's intended best! As the Queen of Sheba said, after seeing Solomon's kingdom, "not even half was told me" (1 Kings 10:7). Poor Mephibosheth (better known as Me-fibbed-sho-nuff—not!) was about to get the surprise of his life. After all, he was living in *abject poverty* with *no hope* of ever changing his *fate*. He had *no future*; just a crippled home life. He was the heir of a king—and a joint-heir besides. Yet there seemed no *hope*, "just more dope," to ease his crippled body! All *hope* seemed to be gone, but still "*these three remain: faith, hope* and *love*"; and as you know, "*love never fails*" (1 Cor. 13:8a,13a).

The covenant God made with Abraham doesn't fail either. You see, God is love. (See Genesis 15:1-18; Deuteronomy 28:1-14; Luke 15:11-32.) Here's the story:

Oh, Mephibosheth! Oh, Lazarus Generation! King David (Jesus) is calling you!

"Who, me?"

Yes, you! Don't be afraid, son!

"Son?"

A Last Word on the Restoration of Lazarus

Yes—son of Jonathan, the son of Saul! Child of God! Joint-heir of *all* things!

"What?"

And Mephibosheth bowed down to pay David (Jesus) honor (praise and worship).

The king said, "Mephibosheth!" The king knew him!

"Your servant!" he replied. The son *knew* his master! Jesus is Lord!

"For I will surely show you kindness (unfailing love and mercy) for the sake of your father, Jonathan, and the covenant."

But show me unfailing kindness like that of the Lord as long as I live, so that I may not be killed, and do not ever cut off your kindness from my family—not even when the Lord has cut off every one of David's enemies from the face of the earth (1 Samuel 20:14-15).

The king says to Mephibosheth, "I will *restore* to you all the land that belonged to Saul, your grandfather. All that land is now yours." Praise the Lord!

Then the king said to Ziba, "And Mephibosheth, grandson of your master, will always eat at my table!" Forevermore!

This Mephibosheth, this Lazarus Generation, is heir of all things through that same covenant of blood.

Jesus paid it all. Let's just bow down and worship at His footstool! He's King of kings and Lord of lords—Lord Jesus!

This last generation, this Lazarus Generation, will be *revived* and *restored*. Just as Lazarus was at the dinner held in Jesus' honor, so you will see this generation feasting forever at King Jesus' table (like David and Mephibosheth). For this is the *will*, the *plan*, and the *purpose* of the Father: to send Jesus to *restore* Lazarus, (Mephibosheth, or America, Africa, Asia, Latin America, Europe, Russia, China, etc.); in short, the whole world and its prodigals! This includes the Church and her prodigals! Rascals, radicals, Lazaruses, Mephibosheths—the restoration of all these things is at hand!

Think about it. Is this the Christ? Is this the One who should come? Both this present Lazarus Generation and the Lazarus of Jesus' time believe that He is the One!

Please hear what our loving heavenly Father is trying to tell us by His precious Holy Spirit: If we don't soon lay down our ecclesiastical cloaks of self-righteousness, our biases and prejudices, our mind sets, our rose-colored glasses that focus only on *our own* denominational fences and fancies… If we don't lay down our own agendas, programs, and personal preferences and together (in unity) as one Body under one Lord, one Spirit, one baptism, and one

A Last Word on the Restoration of Lazarus

Father look on the overripe harvest fields of the world... If we fail to quickly hear the call to prayer and repentance, both corporately and individually... Then we will be *bypassed* by the call of the Spirit that says, "He that hath an ear, let him hear what the Spirit saith unto the *churches* (see Rev. 2–3 KJV). Believe it or not, God will go outside every denomination and camp of the present-day church structure and search for a people who will listen to His heart cry for this lost and dying world! *His heart is turned toward a world that has been ravaged by religion and raped of our morals and minds!*

We must stop warring among ourselves, join the ranks of God's army, and fight the forces of the regions of hell! We either do it or the devil wins our cities, our children, and our churches! Yes, there will be no churches left for us to even "denominationalize" if we don't fight hell together. As His Body, His Bride, His Church—we are built to stand against the "gates of hell." All others are not His Church, only man-made religion. Those all will fall as the shaking continues:

> *See to it that you do not refuse Him who speaks. If they did not escape when they refused him who warned them on earth, how much less will we, if we turn away from Him who warns us from heaven? At the time His voice shook the earth, but now He has promised, "Once more I will shake not only the*

earth but also the heavens." The words "once more" indicate the removing of what can be shaken—that is, created things—so that what cannot be shaken may remain. Therefore, since we are receiving a kingdom that cannot be shaken, let us be thankful, and so worship God acceptably with reverence and awe, for our "God is a consuming fire" (Hebrews 12:25-29).

Chapter 23

Remember Rahab's Red Ribbon?

By the direction of the Holy Spirit I am using here an Old Testament story to prepare, not scare, you for what is about to happen. This is a final warning to us in this Lazarus Generation, the "final" generation before Christ returns and judgment comes upon this world.

Judgment has begun in the house of the Lord. That judgment is for God's people, His Church. "But where shall the ungodly and the sinner appear?" They are mentioned also:

Dear friends, do not be surprised at the painful trial you are suffering, as though something strange were happening to you. But rejoice that you participate in the sufferings of Christ, so that you may be overjoyed when His glory is revealed. If you are insulted because of the name of Christ, you are blessed, for the Spirit of glory and of God rests on you. If you suffer, it should not be as a murderer or thief or any other kind of criminal, or even as a meddler. However, if you suffer as a Christian, do not be ashamed, but praise God that you bear that name. For it is time for judgment to begin with the family of God; and if it begins with us, what will the outcome be for those who do not obey the gospel of God? (1 Peter 4:12-17)

Not so the wicked! They are like chaff that the wind blows away. Therefore the wicked will not stand in the judgment, nor sinners in the assembly of the righteous. For the Lord watches over the way of the righteous, but the way of the wicked will perish (Psalm 1:4-6).

God's judgment upon His people, His chosen ones, could be better stated as God's "discipline" of His people. He disciplines His own, but destroys those who are not His, who are of the world. (See Psalm 94:12-15.) When He speaks of judgment upon the ungodly and sinner, it means just that: total destruction, devastation, and separation from God. It means hell, and then the final judgment—the lake of fire that burns forever (see Rev. 20:15)!

Remember Rahab's Red Ribbon

The Church must be totally *prepared* for what is soon coming upon this earth. That is, we must be either totally prepared or totally scared! Let's choose wisely. Let the wise hear and be saved! *"He that hath an ear, let him hear what the Spirit saith unto the churches."* The Lord is still speaking to the seven types of churches in the Revelation of Jesus Christ. (See chapters 1, 2, and 3 of the Book of Revelation—the "last" book in the Bible.)

I believe the story of Rahab, from an eschatological view, is a true depiction of the actual condition of the Church, the Bride of Christ, at this present time. She represents the adulterous Laodicean church world as recorded in Revelation 3:14-22, a church period that replaces Christ with riches and is bold to justify her adultery and idolatry before the Lord Himself. Jericho also is a true type of our world today, a place ruled by leaders of unbelief. Those leaders are bold to defy and blaspheme the prophets of God and even *God's own Word*! They deny that God can help our present world condition, even if He could make windows in Heaven. So let us view this story of Rahab as representing this present church in a doomed-for-judgment world. In spite of the pending judgment, *there is still hope for Rahab*, the harlot church world, if she does what God says *before it is too late*!

The story of Rahab is found in the Book of Joshua, chapters 2 and 6. Basically, here is what happened.

Moses had died and Joshua was appointed to lead Israel into the Promised Land. So he secretly sent out two spies to "look over the land," especially Jericho. "So they went and entered the house of a *prostitute* named *Rahab* and stayed there" (Josh 2:1b). They actually stayed in a red light district with a rabble-rouser named Rahab. Some would say that God moves in mysterious ways to perform wonders. (That isn't scriptural, but it's a great saying.)

Word had gotten to the King of Jericho that there were spies in the land and city who were there to "check it out" before the great takeover happened. The king sent this message to Rahab: "Bring out the men who came to you and entered your house, because they have come to spy out the whole land" (Josh. 2:3). She had already hidden them, so she replied that the men had been there earlier, but that they left at dusk. "I don't know which way they went. Go after them quickly. You may catch up with them" she said (Josh. 2:5).

She said that she didn't see which way the spies went, and told the king's messengers to go after them! If anyone was in a position for quick death, or "royal suicide," then Rahab was. You just don't lie to the king and live for very long.

What was behind her boldness, brashness, and lack of fear of man? What was behind her "total defiance" to the "powers that be"? It was wisdom. It was fear, not of man, but of Jehovah God. Doesn't the

Remember Rahab's Red Ribbon

Bible say, "The fear of the Lord is the beginning of wisdom"? (See Proverbs 9:10a.)

Before the spies lay down for the night, she went up on the roof and said to them, "I know that the Lord has given this land to you and that a great fear of you has fallen on us, so that all who live in this country are melting in fear because of you. We have heard how the Lord dried up the water of the Red Sea for you when you came out of Egypt, and what you did to Sihon and Og, the two kings of the Amorites east of the Jordan, whom you completely destroyed. When we heard of it, our hearts melted and everyone's courage failed because of you, for the Lord your God is God in heaven above and on the earth below. Now then, please swear to me by the Lord that you will show kindness to my family, because I have shown kindness to you. Give me a sure sign that you will spare the lives of my father and mother, my brothers and sisters, and all who belong to them, and that you will save us from death." "Our lives for your lives!" the men assured her. "If you don't tell what we are doing, we will treat you kindly and faithfully when the Lord gives us the land" (Joshua 2:8-14).

I would say that Rahab was pretty smart (wise). It reminds me of what Jesus said in the New Testament: "Do not be afraid of those who kill the body but cannot kill the soul. Rather, be afraid of the One who can destroy *both* soul and body in hell" (Mt. 10:28).

Keep in mind that Rahab is a type of this Lazarus Generation. Rahab was sinful—totally into adultery and fornication and willing to do almost anything to save herself. But she did not ask to be spared alone when God's army came to take the city (which she knew would happen as a matter of fact). According to the Bible, Rahab said, in effect, "When the God of heaven and earth, who is your God, takes our city and the whole earth, please swear to me by your God (the Lord) that you will show kindness to *my family* because I have shown kindness to you."

What is wisdom? "Do to others as you would have them do to you" (Lk. 6:31). Sow love, reap love. Sow kindness, reap kindness. Sow trust, reap trust. Sow faith, reap eternal life. (See Galatians 6:7.) You can do this not only for yourself, but also for your whole family. "Give me a sure sign [a token] that you will spare the lives of my father and mother, my brothers and sisters, and all who belong to them, and that you will save *us* [not just *me*] from death" (Josh. 2:12c-13). Such unselfishness! Will it go unnoticed and unrewarded simply because she was a harlot?

Could Rahab, the Lazarus Generation of her time, have found a key to being saved? By Lazarus, I mean to be lost without hope and doomed for destruction. Rahab had all of this world's goods, yet was still doomed with her city (a type of this world, a modern Jericho; see Rev. 3:14-22). The whole city, including her family and friends, was doomed for destruction—total destruction. Her Jericho could be the Jericho you live in today—New York City, Los Angeles, San Francisco, Hollywood, Dallas, Denver, Miami, or Washington, D.C.

You may have a successful profession. You may have money, cars, houses, friends, and family. It all doesn't matter; judgment is still coming. Look at the terrorist attack in Manhattan in the spring of 1993. If they had succeeded, nearly 100,000 people would have been destroyed in a moment's time. *The walls of Jericho and the kingdoms of this world are coming down!* The walls of your Jericho and mine—the whole world over—are tumbling to the ground. God's Word said it, so get prepared and not just scared. Walls of pride, lust, fear, and doubt; walls of religions, governments, nations, prejudice, and mind sets; walls of false security (false security in government to protect us and provide safety from everything, from poverty to AIDS)—all walls are coming down! False security in this Laodicean church world will fall also, just as all religion will eventually fall.

Let the wise understand. King Nebuchadnezzar's "mystery statue" made of gold, silver, bronze, iron, and clay is about to come down! The walls are coming down! Every "worldly kingdom" that built its own Jericho with strong and tall walls, with manmade walls, will all come down!

See what Daniel the prophet said:

You looked, O king, and there before you stood a large statue—an enormous, dazzling statue, awesome in appearance. The head of the statue was made of pure gold, its chest and arms of silver, its belly and thighs of bronze, its legs of iron, its feet partly of iron and partly of baked clay. While you were watching, a rock was cut out, but not by human hands. It struck the statue on its feet of iron and clay and smashed them. Then the iron, the clay, the bronze, the silver and the gold were broken to pieces at the same time and became like chaff on a threshing floor in the summer. The wind swept them away without leaving a trace. But the rock that struck the statue became a huge mountain and filled the whole earth (Daniel 2:31-35).

"In the time of those kings, the God of heaven will set up a kingdom that will never be destroyed, nor will it be left to another people. It will crush all those kingdoms and bring them to an end, but it will itself endure forever. This is the meaning of the vision of the rock cut out of a mountain, but not by human hands—a rock that broke the iron, the bronze, the clay, the silver and the gold to pieces. The great God has shown the king what will take place in the future. The dream is true and the interpretation is trustworthy." Then King Nebuchadnezzar fell prostrate before Daniel and paid him honor and ordered that an offering and incense be presented to him. The king said to Daniel, "Surely your God is the God of gods and the Lord of kings and a revealer of mysteries, for you were able to reveal this mystery" (Daniel 2:44-47).

Remember Rahab's Red Ribbon

The walls of Jericho will soon fall again! At that time they were destroyed by God's army, led by Joshua and the priests, followed by the whole nation of Israel, and all directed by Jesus, the Captain of the host of the Lord. Today Jericho will be taken by Jesus, the Rock of our salvation, the Captain of the host of the armies of Heaven! The Lord Himself will lead his armies to battle and bring down the walls of Jericho!

But, what about Rahab? What will be her fate? Her family's fate? Her friends' fate? Her city's fate? Will she and her household be saved? If so, how? Her "token pledge of protection" would not be valid *unless*, when the Israelites entered the land, she *had* (past tense) tied this scarlet cord in the window of her house—the same window through which she let the spies down the wall. Neither would her family be saved unless Rahab had brought her father and mother, brothers and sisters, and all her family *into* her house.

"What? You mean her house, the house of ill repute? Never in a thousand years would I go there to get saved! It's got to be my church, my religion. I can't associate with those kinds of people."

"Don't you know, Lord, that we must go to "such and such" church to get saved? That we must have a sermon, sacrament, song, and then an altar service before we can get saved? Oh, and we must have a catechism by a catechizer who will catechize us for our formal catechistic experience."

Do you know what the Lord's response is? He says, "Huh?" You see, He had never heard of that. Those things are just another wall built by man's religious mind. "Will there be any religious person saved when the walls of religion fall?" Dear reader, don't put your trust, faith, hope, and love in your own religion, denomination, doctrines, or church membership to save you! We are not saved by any of those things. Just because you believe the Bible (God's Word) does not mean you are guaranteed salvation.

So, Rahab had the Word of Truth—and so did the king and all of Jericho! But we are not saved by truth alone. My friend, we are saved by one thing and one thing alone: the scarlet ribbon that Rahab hung in the window of the house of ill repute! That ribbon is a type of the blood. So only by the blood of the Lamb will you and I be saved. In the day of God's judgment, hiding behind the walls of our religious mind sets, beliefs, rituals, church services, beautiful edifices, etc., will not keep us safe. Our offerings and boastings of "a program in the church for every need"; our socials; our fund raisers; our groups; our services—none of these things will save us.

To the angel of the church in Laodicea write: These are the words of the Amen, the faithful and true witness, the ruler of God's creation. I know your deeds, that you are neither cold nor hot. I wish you were either one or the other! So, because you are lukewarm—neither hot nor cold—I am about to spit you out of

My mouth. You say, "I am rich; I have acquired wealth and do not need a thing." But you do not realize that you are wretched, pitiful, poor, blind and naked. I counsel you to buy from Me gold refined in the fire, so you can become rich; and white clothes to wear, so you can cover your shameful nakedness; and salve to put on your eyes, so you can see. Those whom I love I rebuke and discipline. So be earnest, and repent. Here I am! I stand at the door and knock. If anyone hears My voice and opens the door, I will come in and eat with him, and he with Me. To him who overcomes, I will give the right to sit with Me on My throne, just as I overcame and sat down with My Father on His throne. He who has an ear, let him hear what the Spirit says to the churches (Revelation 3:14-22).

Remember, Jesus said in verse 19, "Those whom I love I rebuke and discipline…." Don't forget that.

Rebuke and discipline—that's wisdom!

Rahab (this present church world) may be in adultery, in spiritual or literal fornication, but *she and her whole household can be saved if* she is under the blood at the time judgment comes upon Jericho (this present world order and system). Only by the blood of the Lamb will we be saved.

Then I heard a loud voice in heaven say: "Now have come the salvation and the power and the kingdom of our God, and the authority of His Christ. For the accuser of our brothers, who accuses them before our God day and night, has been hurled down. They overcame him by the blood of the Lamb and by the word of their testimony; they did not love their lives so much as to shrink from death. Therefore rejoice, you heavens and you who dwell in them! But woe to the earth and the sea, because the devil has gone down to you! He is filled with fury, because he knows that his time is short" (Revelation 12:10-12).

Remember the story of David, Jonathan, and Mephibosheth? Mephibosheth (Lazarus) was redeemed (saved, restored) by the blood covenant. So we must make a blood covenant with God, right now! Plead the blood over yourself, your house, your family, your church, your city, your state, your country, and your world!

After all that, Rahab now faces the real task: convincing her family of the coming judgment and total destruction.

Jericho will fall. God Jehovah will do it. His army is now, at this very moment, circling the city. The Lord Himself—Jesus, Commander-in-Chief—Joshua, the priesthood, and the people (the Church) are circling the city.

For six days, once a day, they marched. The trumpets sounded (the prophetic voices spoke). This went on for six thousand years (six days)!

Let the wise understand; these things are warned, prophesied, preached, and proclaimed! Salvation is ours if we repent; judgment is sure if we don't! Remember, Rahab is a type of the church-turned-harlot, a type of our Lazarus Generation. Church, please destroy your walls of doubt, fear, and unbelief...or you will be destroyed by God's army! His Bride today has many lovers, idols, and gods; she has great wealth, but not Christ!

Like the Israelites in Egypt, we need a lamb for a house. Plead the blood! Apply it over the doorposts—the doorposts of your heart and home. "...when He seeth the blood upon the lintel, and on the two side posts, the Lord will pass over the door..." (Ex. 12:23 KJV). It is not when He sees your money, expensive homes, swimming pools, large cars, big savings accounts, church membership card, or church affiliation! It is not when He sees your Holy Bible in your hand. No, it must be written in your holy heart. The Lord said, "when I see the blood" (Ex. 12:13), not "when I see your baptismal certificate"! Neither will He pass over because He sees you sitting in the pew you paid for and that has your brass nameplate on it; nor because you have a good tithing record and sing in the choir. He won't because you are a good Baptist or Pentecostal; a good Catholic or Jew! Only because you are under the blood will He pass over you!

The death angel is coming soon! In fact, it seems he has already begun his "flight of death" over this Egypt, this Jericho. Are you under the protection of the Lamb of God? Are you under His blood? Are you in covenant with Jehovah God? Is your red ribbon hanging in the window of your soul? Rahab, the harlot, had hers ready, and she was saved. The Lazarus people (harlots, etc.) will be saved also, and will likely become some of the greatest evangelists ever. Rahab, the evangelist. Rahab, the righteous! Rahab, the repentant prostitute church world!

Can Rahab convince her family of the coming destruction of Jericho? It won't be easy, for the whole world has seen her harlotry. She did convince them, though.

The seventh time around, when the priests sounded the trumpet blast, Joshua commanded the people, "Shout! For the Lord has given you the city! The city and all that is in it are to be devoted to the Lord. Only Rahab the prostitute and all who are with her in her house shall be spared, because she hid the spies we sent" (Joshua 6:16-17).

But Joshua spared Rahab the prostitute, with her family and all who belonged to her, because she hid the men Joshua had sent as spies to Jericho—and she lives among the Israelites to this day (Joshua 6:25).

She lives among the Israelites to this day! Consider this passage also:

Salmon the father of Boaz, whose mother was Rahab, Boaz the father of Obed, whose mother was Ruth, Obed the father of Jesse, and Jesse the father of King David. David was the father of Solomon, whose mother had been Uriah's wife (Matthew 1:5-6).

Remember Rahab's Red Ribbon

Look at Hebrews 11:30-31 as well:

By faith the walls of Jericho fell, after the people had marched around them for seven days. By faith the prostitute Rahab, because she welcomed the spies, was not killed with those who were disobedient (Hebrews 11:30-31).

She still lives among the Israelites to this day! Hallelujah for Rahab's red ribbon of redemption! Rahab became the mother of Boaz. Boaz and Ruth then had Obed. Obed became the father of Jesse, and Jesse, the father of King David. David was the covenant man (of the blood covenant); he was King of Israel and covenant brother to Jonathan, the father of Mephibosheth (a type of Lazarus).

Get the picture and get under the blood! There is *hope* for the *harlot church*, the Bride of Christ fallen into *spiritual adultery*.

*Peter, an apostle of Jesus Christ, To God's elect, strangers in the world, scattered throughout Pontus, Galatia, Cappadocia, Asia and Bithynia, who have been chosen according to the foreknowledge of God the Father, through **the sanctifying work of the Spirit, for obedience to Jesus Christ and sprinkling by His blood:** Grace and peace be yours in abundance. Praise be to the God and Father of our Lord Jesus Christ! In His great mercy He has given us new birth into a living hope through the resurrection of Jesus Christ from the dead, and into* *an inheritance that can never perish, spoil or fade—kept in heaven for you, who through faith are shielded by God's power until the coming of the **salvation that is ready to be revealed in the last time**. In this you greatly rejoice, though now for a little while you may have had to suffer grief in all kinds of trials. These have come so that your faith—of greater worth than gold, which perishes even though refined by fire—may be proved genuine and may result in praise, glory and honor when Jesus Christ is revealed. Though you have not seen Him, you love Him; and even though you do not see Him now, you believe in Him and are filled with an inexpressible and glorious joy, for you are receiving the goal of your faith, the salvation of your souls* (1 Peter 1:1-9).

Let's allow the sanctifying work of the Spirit to cleanse us from all spiritual adultery and harlotry. Let's be obedient to live under the blood. *Our only hope is in the resurrection power of Jesus to save and keep us until His soon coming*! There is *hope* for Rahab, this harlot church world. So quickly *repent* and *return* to Christ and His cleansing blood. (See my first book, *Run, Satan, Run—But You Can't Hide!* for a look at the complete sanctification we need in these last days in order to be ready for Christ's coming.)

Chapter 24

The Finished Product

Let's close with a final illustration of the Lazarus Generation message. This Lazarus Generation message is the heart and soul of this book. Perhaps this will help relieve the burning in my soul and spirit of this great revelation and urgent message from God, as we near the end of this present age.

Let's go to the Scriptures. It is in the Word that we learn of Him, and so have faith in Him. Turn to the Gospel of John, chapter 4. No greater or purer example regarding the Lazarus Generation can be found than in this passage. It is a story of what was, what is, and what will be. In order to build your faith, I am providing the entire account. This is your final opportunity to see and be wise before it is too late!

The Pharisees heard that Jesus was gaining and baptizing more disciples than John, although in fact it was not Jesus who baptized, but His disciples. When the Lord learned of this, He left Judea and went back once more to Galilee. Now He had to go through Samaria. So He came to a town in Samaria called Sychar, near the plot of ground Jacob had given to his son Joseph. Jacob's well was there, and Jesus, tired as He was from the journey, sat down by the well. It was about the sixth hour. When a Samaritan woman came to draw water, Jesus said to her, "Will you give Me a drink?" (His disciples had gone into the town to buy food.) The Samaritan woman said to Him, "You are a Jew and I am a Samaritan woman. How can You ask me for a drink?" (For Jews do not associate with Samaritans.) Jesus answered her, "If you knew the gift of God and who it is that asks you for a drink, you would have asked Him and He would have given you living water." "Sir," the woman said, "You have nothing to draw with and the well is deep. Where can You get this living water? Are You greater than our father Jacob, who gave us the well and drank from it himself, as did also his sons and his flocks and herds?" Jesus answered, "Everyone who drinks this water will be thirsty again, but whoever drinks the water I give him will never thirst. Indeed, the water I give him will become in him a spring of water welling up to eternal life." The woman said to Him, "Sir, give me this water so that I won't get thirsty and have to keep coming here to draw water." He told her, "Go, call your husband and come back." "I have no husband," she replied. Jesus said to her, "You are right when you say you have no husband. The fact is, you have had five husbands, and the man you now have is not your husband. What you have just said is quite true." "Sir," the woman said, "I can see that You are a prophet. Our fathers worshiped on this mountain, but you Jews claim that the place where we must worship is in Jerusalem." Jesus declared, "Believe Me, woman, a time is coming when you will worship the Father neither on this mountain nor in Jerusalem. You Samaritans worship what you do not know; we worship what we do know, for salvation is from the Jews. Yet a time is coming and has now come when the true worshipers will worship the Father in spirit and truth, for they are the kind of worshipers the Father seeks. God is spirit, and His worshipers must worship in spirit and in truth." The woman said, "I know that Messiah" (called Christ) "is coming. When He comes, He will explain everything to us." Then Jesus declared, "I who speak to you am He." Just then His disciples returned and were surprised to find Him talking with a woman. But no one asked, "What do You want?" or "Why are You talking with her?" Then, leaving her water jar, the woman went back to the town and said to the people, "Come, see a man who told me everything I ever did. Could this be the Christ?" They came out of the town and made their way toward Him. Meanwhile His disciples urged Him, "Rabbi, eat something." But He said to them,

"I have food to eat that you know nothing about." Then His disciples said to each other. "Could someone have brought Him food?" "My food," said Jesus, "is to do the will of Him who sent Me and to finish His work. Do you not say, 'Four months more and then the harvest'? I tell you, open your eyes and look at the fields! They are ripe for harvest. Even now the reaper draws his wages, even now he harvests the crop for eternal life, so that the sower and the reaper may be glad together. Thus the saying, 'One sows and another reaps' is true. I sent you to reap what you have not worked for. Others have done the hard work, and you have reaped the benefits of their labor." Many of the Samaritans from that town believed in Him because of the woman's testimony, "He told me everything I ever did." So when the Samaritans came to Him, they urged Him to stay with them, and He stayed two days. And because of His words many more became believers. They said to the woman, "We no longer believe just because of what you said; now we have heard for ourselves, and we know that this man really is the Savior of the world" (John 4:1-42).

No one in any generation, be it Old Testament, New Testament, or the present, speaks so clearly to us of this Lazarus Generation as does this portion of Scripture. No other presents so well its condition and *its hope*. This great hope is only in Jesus Christ and in faith in His blood—the blood we apply in making a blood covenant with Him. Only by appling the blood can we truly be saved!

The Finished Product

Let me paraphrase the story of the Samaritan woman in order to make my point and give some final remarks about this last generation.

Jesus' earthly ministry was picking up great momentum. He was having more converts and baptisms than His cousin, John. John's disciples and the Jews were in an argument over the matter of, as you might have guessed, "ceremonial washing," or religion, pure and simple (see John 3:25). As chapter 4 of John's Gospel begins, we see that the Pharisees got wind of this argument and jumped on the band wagon, so to speak.

At this point Jesus left the country. He didn't like "religion" then and He doesn't like it today. (Today's religious arguments are greater, though.) The religious church structure of the day was doing business as usual: They fought among themselves while the people were dying in their sins and going to hell in a hand basket. All the time the harvest got riper each day and the Messiah, the Lord Himself, walked in their midst.

No doubt Jesus was totally disgusted with their religions, bigotry, biased mind sets, and prideful prejudices. So He told His disciples, "I've got to go through Samaria."

"You, the Master, go through the dirty dog Samaritans' territory? I can't believe it, Lord!"

Jesus journeyed until He reached a town called Sychar where there was a well that Jacob had dug. Tired from the journey, Jesus sat down by the well. It was around noon, and His disciples were in the city getting food.

That was the introduction; afterwards we see the real reason Jesus came to earth, lived here, hung on a cross, and rose from the dead. He did it for the Lazarus people, not for the religious. It was not to start another sect, synagogue, or social club; it was to call sinners to repentance. (I think He meant to call the "self-righteous" to repentance.)

*As Jesus went on from there, He saw a man named Matthew sitting at the tax collector's booth. "Follow Me," He told him, and Matthew got up and followed Him. While Jesus was having dinner at Matthew's house, many tax collectors and "sinners" came and ate with Him and His disciples. When the Pharisees saw this, they asked His disciples, "Why does your teacher eat with tax collectors and 'sinners'?" On hearing this, Jesus said, "It is not the healthy who need a doctor, **but the sick**. But go and learn what this means: '**I desire mercy**, not **sacrifice**.' For I have not come to call the **righteous**, but **sinners**"* (Matthew 9:9-13).

Let's take a look at who He is talking to and the results of that conversation.

First of all, Jesus was talking to a woman, and a Samaritan woman at that. At that time, Samaritans were considered dogs. In the eyes of the Jews,

Samaritans had no soul and no hope of salvation. (They were wrong!)

"Lord, if You are going to practice your personal evangelism skills, please do it on a *man*, not a *woman*! And look at the woman You chose—she's a prostitute! A Samaritan prostitute! She's had five husbands and is living with the sixth man! What will our church folks think? What will Your organization's overseers say? You might lose your preaching papers, Lord, by associating with such low life. You of all people, Lord, should know that Jews don't associate with Samaritans (Gentiles)."

Jesus not only talked to her, which was forbidden, but He also asked her for a drink of water. That was totally unacceptable! Even the woman said, "You're a Jew and I'm a Samaritan."

Jesus then astounded her with this reply: "If you only know who I am and what God's gift of grace is to you, you would be asking Me for a drink and I would give to you a drink of water you would never forget—living water!"

"That sounds read good, Lord, but where does it come from? You don't have a rope and this well is deep. By the way, do You think You are better than our father, Jacob? He drank here, and so did his sons and their flocks."

What did she mean? She said, in effect, "You come here to our territory, our city, and our well, and tell us how to find living water. If Jacob couldn't do it, how can You, a Jew, do it?"

Even more basic, she said, "I don't see that you Jews have any more going for you in meeting needs, problems, etc., than we Samaritans do in our religion and traditions."

She was right. Circumcision or no circumcision, it profited nothing! Religion is not the answer. Jesus, however, didn't let her challenge stop Him. He knew He had caught her attention and aroused her curiosity. So He just replied with this life-giving line: "Everyone [Jew or Gentile] who drinks this water will be thirsty again, but whoever drinks the water I give him *will never thirst.*"

This water will become a spring of water—not just a well. It will well up, spring up, to eternal life. It's everlasting life! It has a beginning but will last forever—eternally yours.

"Sir," she said to Jesus, "give me this water. Quickly! Then I won't get thirsty and have to come here in the heat of the day in order to avoid all those other women who look down on me for what I do and am."

"Go, get your husband, and then come back."

Can you imagine what she was thinking? "Oh no! I knew it. They just don't stop. I knew there was a catch somewhere. I had my hopes up for nothing.

The Finished Product

So the woman replied, "I don't have a husband, sir."

"You're right," Jesus said. "You've had five and are now just living with a man."

"He too has heard what I am," she thinks. "There is just *too much past* to forgive. There's too much sin even for this prophet of God. I know He's a prophet, but we have always had the prophets. They tell me what's wrong but don't give me any way out of my sordid life style."

The woman looks at Jesus. "Sir, I worship on this mountain. I do the best I can. You Jews say that we must worship in Jerusalem. Well, I would go to Your church, except I'm not welcome. I'm not good enough. So if I must go to Your church and worship there in Jerusalem, I guess I will never get that living water You speak of. I'm just doomed to hell, sir. I'm not allowed into Your group for so many reasons—money, social status, clothing, location, doctrine, denominational barriers, rules....

"I'd love to sing and dance for the Lord Jehovah, but with all these past divorces and things, I know I wouldn't be accepted in Your church. Perish the thought that I might teach or hold a respectable position there. I can pay my tithes, attend a class for new converts, get baptized in water, and if I am real good for a while, I might just get to join the church. But I'd never be allowed to preach or teach. I wouldn't be considered good enough to be ordained or licensed to pastor, or to be an evangelist or a missionary, or something like that.

"Could I just sweep the church floor and clean the bathroom, sir? Yes! Oh, I would be glad to! But what if God asked me to preach? Could I be ordained in Your church, sir? Would my past hinder me?" (If the New Testament had been written then, she might have added, "Oh, I guess the Bible didn't mean what it said, sir, 'Therefore, if anyone is in Christ, he is a new creation; the old has gone, the new has come!' " [See Second Corinthians 5:17.])

This is what Jesus said:

"Believe Me, woman, a time is coming when you, a Samaritan, will worship the Father not in a Gentile or Jewish religion, but as a true worshiper!

"You worship now what you do not know. You have only one part of worship. You worship in your spirit, but you don't know the truth yet. Worship in spirit alone is not enough. On the other hand, we Jews know who we should worship, but that too is not enough. We have the truth (a form of worship) but no life. You have the lively spirit of worship but no truth.

"Ah, but the time is coming and—get ready, dear sister—the time is coming and now is when the true (real) worshipers will worship in spirit and in truth!

"God the Father, Jehovah God, whom you seek to worship as a Gentile, is Spirit. He seeks His true worshipers and they *must* worship in spirit and in truth!"

Wow! Here is the real Messiah!

"I may be a Samaritan and I may be a woman. I may be a real sinner; I may be a prostitute. I may have a bad reputation in society, but I know truth when I hear it. I know *hope* when I see it! And I know what Moses and the prophets say about the true Messiah. I know He is coming and when He does, He will explain everything to us. I also know that He is not religious, biased, bigoted, or unforgiving.

"Finally, I've found Him! Oh joy! He knows me—through and through—yet He still loves me! He loves me as I am. I didn't find Him at a certain church either. I found Him at my point of need! It could have been anywhere: at the well, a wall, a hall, or a mall! In a hole or dive; in a home alone. It's all in the heart. I don't need a place called holy by man. I found the Messiah not in a sacred shrine, but in this heart of mine!

"I've got to tell somebody what Jesus did for me!"

Then she left her water pot behind. That act speaks volumes. Earthly cares, heartaches, the past, an old life style—you name it, it's gone! Soul ties, religious spirits, and separate camps are all forgotten. There's neither Jew nor Gentile. It's just Jesus!

Who gave this woman authority? Who signed her ordination papers? Who called her?

She didn't have any other person's approval; Jesus touched her, loved her, forgave her, cleansed her, and covered her with His blood covenant! She cut a covenant with the Lord.

"You gave me living water; I give You my life, for as long as I live. You witnessed to me; I'll witness for You! You chose me; I choose You too. You loved me when I was unlovable; I love You forever.

"I've got to tell somebody. I've got to tell somebody what He has done for me! Hey! Sychar! Come see Jesus!"

This Samaritan woman became a real live evangelist. She won a whole city for Christ—and did it without formal religion or its approval!

Then the disciples arrived on the scene. "Master, please eat!"

"I have food, boys, that you, My own disciples, know nothing about."

"What? Who gave this food to You?"

"My food," said Jesus, "is to do the will of the Father and finish His work, not My work; His will, not My will."

What is the will of God?

It's to seek and save the lost at any cost, even to death!

"You boys are My disciples, that is true. But you have missed the point. You still seek food for your stomachs first. You satisfy your creature comforts first. You see with the natural eyes. But I say look on the fields. With your eyes you think there are four more months until we will harvest some more bread"—money, cars, buildings, salaries, checking accounts, bigger crowds, popularity.

No! You've missed it, disciples, twenty-first century church world. Jesus was simply speaking of the Lazarus harvest. Lazarus is dead in trespass and sins; the fields, the lost people, are white unto harvest! Let's reap while it is day, for night cometh when no man can reap! The world's harvest is ripe and *over ready* for harvesting. How can we sit around playing church, and fiddling with toys, (boys)?

No vision—just television!

No prayer—just a lot of hot air!

No repentance—just more religion!

No unity—just more division!

If we, meaning organized religion, don't get it together soon, Jesus *will* say, "I've had enough of you Pharisees and you, John's disciples, arguing over matters of ceremonial washing (religion). I've had enough of you church pillars (unmovable objects). I've had enough of your closed attitudes where people go to purgatory if they don't believe like you do." Jesus will just say, "I must go to Samaria." He will go win a Lazarus Generation to do His work for Him, and they will get the job done too! Don't think that just because you're this or that, God won't leave you sitting in your pew.

Wake up or get left behind in this, the greatest hour of the Church!

The world awaits Jesus, not religion!

Lazarus will take Him to the world, whether or not you do.

Lazarus, come forth in Jesus' name!

Now loose him and let him go! Praise the Lord!

To the angel of the church in Laodicea write: These are the words of the Amen, the faithful and true witness, the ruler of God's creation. I know your deeds, that you are neither cold nor hot. I wish you were either one or the other! **So, because you are lukewarm— neither hot nor cold—I am about to spit you out of My mouth.** *You say, "I am rich; I have acquired wealth and do not need a thing." But you do not realize that you are wretched, pitiful, poor, blind and naked. I counsel you to buy from Me gold refined in the fire, so you can become rich; and white clothes to wear, so you can cover your shameful nakedness; and salve to put on your eyes, so you can see.* **Those whom I love I rebuke and discipline.** *So be earnest, and repent. Here I am! I stand at the door and knock. If anyone hears My voice and opens the door, I will come in and eat with him, and he with Me. To him who overcomes, I will give the* *right to sit with Me on My throne, just as I overcame and sat down with My Father on His throne. He who has an ear, let him hear what the Spirit says to the churches* (Revelation 3:14-22).

Here in these few verses Jesus makes His final appeal to this present Laodicean church period. He pleads for us to heed His counsel, to repent and be *spiritually prepared* to minister to this *final* generation. Otherwise He will surely *bypass* this Laodicean church and raise up a *new movement*, one where the people will listen to Him, *repent*, and do His bidding.

So let's return to *intimacy* with Christ. Let's *repent* of our idolatry! The alternative is to be spit out of the mouth of Jesus as a lukewarm, putrid, foul-tasting, backslidden religious body. Our religion-ridden church world is blinded by self-comfort and gratification. We think prosperity, worldly goods, or financial wealth will be enough to merit God's blessings and *grace* to reach a lost and dying world. Friends, that won't work. Money will not cover our spiritual nakedness. Worldly success will not help save this Lazarus Generation. Only Jesus and His *true* Bride (the true Church) can reach this lost and dying generation. It will take God's love (not the lottery). It is through *righteousness*, not riches!

Wake up, O Laodicean church! Seek the Lord while He may be found or be spit out and passed by.

If Jesus said He would do it, then He will. We can't afford to play games anymore. Heed the call of the Spirit today! We have a great work to do. The Lazarus Generation awaits us—and so does Jesus. Open the door and let Him in His Church so He can revive us!

To contact Samuel Brassfield for speaking engagements or to order additional copies of *The Lazarus Generation* or *Run, Satan, Run—But You Can't Hide*, write or call:

Harvest International Ministries (H.I.M.)
140 N. Mesa, Suite 3
Fruita, CO 81521

Phone:	303-858-4340
FAX:	303-858-7473